HOKKAIDO
北海道
■ **SAPPORO** 札幌

● MORIOKA 盛岡

● YAMAGATA 山形

● NIIGATA 新潟
HONSHU
本州

● NAGANO 長野

● KANAZAWA 金沢

TAKAYAMA 高山

NORTH PACIFIC OCEAN
北太平洋

■ **TOKYO** 東京
● YOKOHAMA 横浜

KYOTO 京都
▲ Mount Fuji
富士山

■ ● NARA 奈良
■ **OSAKA** 大阪
▲
Mount Koya 高野山

KEY

■ Major city
● Town
▲ Mountain

MINDFULNESS

—

TRAVEL

—

JAPAN

NATURE, FOOD, FOREST BATHING, TEA CEREMONIES,
ONSEN, CRAFT & MEDITATION

Steve Wide and
Michelle Mackintosh

Hardie Grant

EXPLORE

C
O
N
T
E
N
T
S

CONTENTS

THE ZEN OF THINGS

Be not afraid of going slowly,
be afraid of standing still
– Japanese Proverb

We wake to the smell of green tea, grilled fish and the scent of wood and tatami. The morning light throws shadows on the shoji screens of our ryokan (traditional Japanese inn) room. Our breakfast is booked for 8am so we float out of bed, put on our yukata (robe), tabi (socks) and zōri (sandals) and make our way along the long, narrow corridor to the breakfast room. Tiny snowflakes drift lazily from the sky and ice clings to the windows, although the day looks bright and clear.

Our waiter appears with a pot of hojicha (tea) and small glasses of local apple juice (the Yudanaka area is famous for its apples). Artful dishes appear at our table – mountain vegetables, a perfectly cooked egg, grilled fish, pickles and rice, and a tiny dish of yoghurt and fresh fruit. It looks almost as if there is too much food but each dish is perfectly portioned and complements the next.

We plan our day over breakfast, making sure we leave spaces in-between, a Japanese philosophy called 'ma' that we always like to build into our travel. We head back to our room to gather our onsen kit (towels, toiletries and hairbrush) and make our way to the Momoyama Bath (a Cultural Tangible Property) that was built in the Edo period (1603 to 1867). One entrance has blue linen noren curtains with the Kanji for man 男 and one has the pinky red linen noren with the Kanji for women 女. The baths rotate from night to day so we are able to partake in both bathing experiences.

The night before, Michelle had had one of the best baths of her life. It was an exquisite, large and softly lit rotenburo (outside bath) with a formal garden. 'Modesty rocks' were placed about the pool so she almost felt alone under the stars, bathing in the warm yellow light of the lanterns while she marvelled at the breathtaking view back onto the historic wooden façade of the building. As the steam rose from the volcanic water, soft snow fell on her head and shoulders. She shut her eyes whilst soaking her travel-weary body, feeling every stress and thought leave her mind and body and float into the ether.

Now it was Steve's turn. He drifted through the noren (linen curtains) and put his clothes and cares into the locker. Outside, the winter air was bracing. Sinking into the hot water and gazing out onto a lush garden accented by a large stone lantern, he enjoyed the perfect bath. Later we met back in our room with stories of our bathing experiences.

Our morning has set the tone for our day. We tread softly, noticing each step on our path. We observe the vivid green of the winter forest's leaves, the powdery crunch of the snow, and at lunch the deep darks of the lacquerware our miso soup is held in and the rustic textural pottery of our teacups. We speak of how the light diffuses through the leaves of the trees. We are mindful of those who have trod the path before us. When our plans hit an obstacle, we simply acknowledge the change and move forward – knowing we are about to embrace another unexpected adventure.

This is our Japan.

J A P A N E S E P H I L O S O P H Y

Japan has taught us how we would like to live in the world. It has taught us to see travel through a new lens, to cultivate a love of everyday beauty and an appreciation for nature and her seasons, of blossoms, leaves and snowflakes. Small things like taking time out of our day for quiet reflection over a cup of tea or gentle observance of the way the light shapes the shadows around us are now intrinsically entwined in the way we live when we're at home.

The Buddhist and Shinto beliefs at the core of Japanese society talk of a connection to nature and that everything is transient. The underpinning beliefs encourage us all to be kind and compassionate; to practise simplicity and reflection; to live and love completely; and notice all the small things while travelling on our path.

Understanding contemporary Japan lies in finding the essence of ancient Japanese culture by travelling to small communities and walking and cycling around the backstreets. It's about stopping for chance connections and trying to live like a local. What has gone before defines and shapes the present in Japan. Bold graphic prints on kimono reflect updated modernism. The design of a robot could be shaped by Zen philosophy. What might look to the Western eye unfinished or unobserved is a meticulously thought-out idea. It's a country so deeply layered that as outsiders we have only absorbed a tiny fraction of the possibilities.

Japan celebrates a culture that reveres moon viewing, marks the changing of the seasons with festivities, eats seasonally and has unbelievable nature, from shinrin yoku (forest bathing) to towns and cities with beautiful green spaces and immaculately kept gardens. Trains are fast and efficient, communal onsen (hot springs) and sento (regular water bath) bathing is affordable and relaxing to all, and pilgrimage paths that were tramped centuries ago are still being walked today. Silence is in the everyday. Calm is in the rapidly beating hearts of the cities.

This is the way of things in Japan. This is the true art of mindfulness. Walk with us as we show you our favourite experiences, moments and places. Stay close and tread lightly.

WORK/LIFE BALANCE AND THE INFLUENCE OF TRAVEL

Everyone seems to be working harder and longer. With mobile phones and tablets, work seeps into our leisure time, our nights and our weekends. It's hard to escape from emails and phone calls and never-ending deadlines. When we cannot slow down and our lives won't permit a timeout for a mindful experience, our wiring can get crossed. Thought processes slow down, empathy wanes, productivity is reduced and our overall contentedness with life, and appreciation and enjoyment of it, is damaged. We lose what it is to be ourselves.

In times of modernism, change and development, Western societies have missed the opportunity to create their own template for mindfulness. As a result, we have often looked to Eastern philosophies for ideas on how to be truly mindful. The West has plundered ideas from across the globe and incorporated religions and practices from different cultures into quests for a mindful approach that fits lifestyles and can be part of contemporary work/life balance.

Mindfulness takes in a range of ideas: wellness treatments, philosophies, religious beliefs, pampering, food, exercise and much more – but ultimately it deals with the central idea of taking note of your surroundings, being present in the moment and being aware of the natural and spiritual pleasures of slowing down, taking your time and allowing everyday healing to diffuse into your body and soul.

Mindfulness is woven into the fabric of everyday life in Japan. It's practised in the tea ceremony, onsen (hot springs) bathing, calligraphy, ikebana, meditation practices, shinrin yoku (forest bathing). It can also be found in temple and ryokan (traditional Japanese inn) stays and Buddhist vegetarian shojin ryori (vegetarian banquet) feasts that are natural, simple and healthy and yet convey a true sense of luxury and indulgence. Gardens and parks are designed spaces where visitors can absorb the true beauty of the seasons. Planting and placement allows for tranquil and inspiring strolls. Slowing down and taking stock of your surroundings, appreciating the beauty in nature and the everyday and assessing your place within the world – it's all part of the Japanese approach to life.

Travelling in Japan unlocks experiences which help you gain a deeper understanding of what it is to be mindful. Then, in keeping your travel experiences close to your heart, you can bring Japanese mindfulness into your everyday life.

Planning a trip can be both exciting and daunting. We always travel to Japan with a particular adventure in mind. Visiting a prefecture known for food, onsen (hot springs) or craft, or booking a trip to see blossoms or falling leaves. A friend's birthday, Christmas in Japan, an exhibition. You could travel with one of our chapters in mind, perhaps creative classes, forest bathing, or to walk one of the pilgrimage trails. Plan ahead, check the weather, choose a season that suits you.

A holiday in Japan is full of the unfamiliar. A non-English-speaking country with different foods and transport systems. It's quite easy to feel stressed when things don't go to plan. Therefore, building a few dedicated times for quiet reflection can help you brave the unexpected. Stop for a cup of tea and shut your eyes for a few moments. Collect your thoughts by sitting on a park bench in a garden or quiet place. Think before speaking. Don't fill gaps in conversation, speak confidently and quietly when you need to.

Be mindful to slow down, change pace from your frenetic work self. Make time for yourself, declutter your mind. A good holiday should leave you feeling refreshed, relaxed and inspired. It will give you time to think about your life, take stock of things. It should be a circuit-breaker. A good holiday should help you reassess what is important to you. Of course, there is no better place than Japan to have this kind of holiday.

Most of all, start your holiday in your mind before you go. You can build the anticipation and structure an itinerary but always remember that the adventures that go off schedule can be the ones that stay with you forever.

ON SELF-CARE POETRY AND NATURE

Self-care is key to happiness and peacefulness. Taking care of yourself can be as simple as making time for a micro meditation, wandering around a garden or through a forest. A pocketbook of short-form haiku poetry is a perfect travel companion. Contemplating a poem a day will help your mind relax and bring focus to your travel. As you read through these pages, we hope some of the experiences and activities we share will spark your imagination and lead you on a path to planning the mindful trip you deserve.

ON SILENCE AND STILLNESS

In Western culture we love to talk. This is in stark contrast to Japan where it is more polite to speak fewer words in a softer voice. Japanese people convey tone and feelings through body language and other non-verbal communication (refer to the concept of Yugen on p. 15). Mindfulness of others in public spaces is a key to learning how to experience the best Japanese holiday. It is often said that in the West we are a singular society and Japan is a collective society. For example, the shoji screen was invented to promote quiet talking, so as not to disturb those in other rooms (literally through paper-thin walls). So when you're in Japan, adopt the collective consciousness and always be mindful of others.

One of the key principles of Zen Buddhism is silent contemplation. Absorbing culture through listening and observing can be integral to appreciating your new surroundings when travelling. To be silent is to take a break from oneself, hear your

inner voice, empty your mind from all the swirling thoughts. Many of the best mindful experiences in Japan are conducive to silence or very few words. Onsen (hot springs) bathing, experiencing the tea ceremony, shinrin yoku (forest bathing), meditation, Buddhist retreats and more.

A SOLO HOLIDAY

There is a beautiful melancholy to spending time alone. Getting lost in your own thoughts and limiting the moments each day talking to others gives your mind a break from the constant clutter of daily communication. Books you've been dying to read, new places you've been wanting to visit, getting lost, then being found.

Shut your eyes and imagine you are the poet Basho wandering the crooked Edo-period (1603 to 1867) paths, or perhaps you are a character in Kawabata's *Snow Country*, shut off for the winter in the snowy north. Maybe you're in a candlelit room admiring the light play in Tanizaki's *In Praise of Shadows*. You'll begin to notice life's subtleties: the smell of incense in the air, the fresh clarity rain brings, the sun breaking through the troubled skies over stormy mountains.

A STREAM-OF-CONSCIOUSNESS HOLIDAY

Book your accommodation, research how to get there from the airport, then spend your holiday walking or cycling to places near where you are staying. Go where the weather and the path you're on takes you. Rest when your body feels tired, eat when you are hungry. On this kind of holiday, you will meet more locals, feel the cycle of the day more keenly and learn to listen to what your body wants and needs. We always leave at least a few days to practise this ritual but until writing this book we'd never put a name to it.

For us, this practice is about finding the real Japan, meeting people going about their daily routines. Try this in a small town, somewhere out of the way and not on the tourist trail. Let the movements of your mind dictate your direction and you'll discover things about yourself you hadn't noticed.

DEVISE YOUR OWN TRAVEL RITUALS

For us, travelling to Japan is a mixture of being curious for new adventures and revisiting and building on our favourite things to do. We pack light, always include nature, art and culture in our itinerary and almost exclusively eat Japanese food. We take a long break in our day for a good cup of tea, and try and learn as many new Japanese words as we can. We make sure our travel route is comfortable and not rushed and we book most of our Japan Rail Pass train rides in the first few days. If we are anywhere near a good sento (regular water bath) or onsen (hot springs), going for a soak is non-negotiable.

Your rituals will be different to ours but the most important thing is to think about what you'd like your trip to look like and not put too much pressure on yourself to do absolutely everything on your list. It's important you have a gentle holiday fitting in what you can.

CONDUCT A MICRO TIDY OF THE MIND

Spend each day before your trip removing all unnecessary baggage so your mind travels light (and can now fit in the overhead compartment). This is the key to successfully travelling in Japan. Delete and trash unwanted thoughts and feelings. Top up with pre-trip reading (*see* our tips opposite) and dreams of the weeks to come. If any negativity, anxiety or fear pops into your mind, delete the trash straight away.

PACK A CAPSULE WARDROBE

Your clothing should be seasonally driven and minimal in nature. We offer these tips:

· Neutral colours can be mixed and matched to make new and interesting outfit ensembles.

· Pack breathable and natural fabrics, such as linens, cottons, wool and cashmere.

· You might like to pack coloured patterned scarves, tops or jackets that can be layered or swapped around to create a new outfit.

· Only take a cabin-size bag to make it easy for yourself getting on trains and walking to hotels. You'll save on your carbon footprint or expenses by avoiding taxis and Ubers too.

· You can steam the crinkles out of your clothing in the bathroom whilst you take a shower or, like Michelle, you might prefer to wear your linen clothing naturally crinkled.

· Tech is heavy and can take up space. Work out what you will need to take with you and go for lighter options.

BOOKS TO READ

- *Oku no Hosomichi: The Narrow Road to the Interior* by Matsuo Basho
- *Between the Floating Mist: Poems of Ryokan* by Ryokan
- *In Praise of Shadows* by Jun'ichirō Tanizaki
- *The Book of Tea* by Okakura Kakuzo
- *Goodbye, Things* by Fumio Sasaki
- *Wabi Sabi* by Beth Kempton
- *Writings from the Zen Masters*, Penguin books – Great Ideas.

RESEARCH

- Organise or research your best airport transportation (times, platforms, prices). The more detail you have beforehand, the faster you can move through airports, which helps a lot after a long flight. It also means you don't look lost when you arrive.
- Plan the best plane attire for you. We always wear something that is both comfortable and presentable for arrival or change before we land into something chic. Looking good makes you feel confident – and that leads to a spring in your step and a better trip.

THE WEEK BEFORE YOU LEAVE

- Take your suitcase out and pack in stages. A capsule wardrobe with pieces that go together will not only keep your suitcase light but give you more sartorial options (*see* opposite page).
- If you can pre-order your plane food do so. Order a Japanese option if possible to get you in the mood!
- Pack your carry-on bag early so that you're not stressing about it the day before you leave! We recommend a carry-on with lots of compartments and suggest you pack the following:
  - A plethora of music, movies and podcasts to listen to.
  - A journal to write or draw in.
  - Passport and tickets.
  - An actual camera is nicer to use than a phone.
  - Noise-cancelling headphones or ear buds.
  - Something to rest your head on. A blow-up pillow or a thick scarf or jumper.
  - Cosy socks and an eye mask.
  - A small toiletries bag for freshening up during the flight.

THE DAY BEFORE YOU LEAVE

- Eat something clean.
- Stay away from booze.
- Try and get the best sleep you can.
- Pack your own snacks. Nut mix, rice crackers, favourite homemade snacks could save your life if the plane food is not to your liking.
- Pack anything not already in your carry-on, like your wallet.
- Make time for a bit of pampering, a facemask, bath, anything you find relaxing.
- Check your flight is on schedule.
- Leave a copy of your passport and itinerary and a set of keys with a trusted friend, in case someone needs to access your place while you're away.
- Set up an email reply letting work colleagues and friends know you will be away and not answering correspondence.
- Turn your tech off for a few hours to give yourself a bit of quiet time to mentally prepare.
- Don't pack your emotional baggage.

SENOBI BREATHING

Senobi is a deep-breathing technique associated with stretching. It activates the nervous system, regulates hormones and is said to be good for heart health. Practise this technique for prevention of nerves each night in the hotel and to decompress when you get home. Have a look on YouTube for a teacher and technique that suits you.

AT THE AIRPORT

· Get to the airport early so you are not rushing or stressing.
· However, as you make your way to the airport sneak in a few deep breaths. Shut your eyes and breathe in and count to five, breathe out and count to three. Or meditate on a word, phrase or song that means something to you.
· Be prepared for crowds, delays and mishaps. Have a relaxation technique ready to use if unexpected things arise.
· Try not to eat anything heavy before you get on the plane. Eat something fresh like salad or fruit and then eat less on the plane.

ON THE PLANE

Michelle needs all the cosy things around her and she loves to stay analogue, preferring to write and draw in her journal – rather than listen to music or watch movies. She always brings her own snacks and wears a 'convertible outfit' – something to get on and off the plane with that cuts a fine figure but converts to something more comfortable whilst sitting on the plane.

Meanwhile, Steve gets into his own 'plane bubble' (it's a separate universe in between the two worlds of home and holiday while in the air). Ambient music (Brian Eno, Ólafur Arnalds and Nils Frahm are all good choices or even meditation soundtracks), books, writing and films. He always starts with a 'healthy' Bloody Mary and makes sure his meal is pre-ordered so as to avoid disappointment.

TIPS FOR BEING CALM ON THE PLANE

· Be equipped with noise-cancelling headphones or ear buds.
· Memorise where you have put things in your carry-on bag pockets, so you are not rummaging or getting up and down opening the overhead locker every hour.
· Drink lots of water – hydration will help you feel refreshed when you land.
· Practise your favourite meditation or breathing techniques intermittently.
· Cast your mind (far) away from the inelegance of a plane toilet or the economy seating arrangements.

TIPS FOR GETTING A GOOD SLEEP ON THE PLANE

· Don't drink much or any alcohol on the plane. Instead, order a green, mint or chamomile tea to help relaxation.
· Don't eat too much.
· Choose clean, lean food options.
· Rest your head on a travel pillow or a thick scarf or jumper.
· Wear cosy socks, an eye mask and put your ear plugs in and listen to relaxing music on your device.
· Practise some deep breathing.
· Remember micro sleeps and power naps are important relaxation techniques.

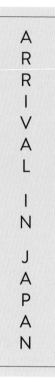

A
R
R
I
V
A
L

I
N

J
A
P
A
N

Because you've planned your transportation ahead (*see* p. 7), you can hopefully move quickly through the airport and arrival gates. It always feels great to arrive, but this is not the fun part of your trip. Try to take your planned mode of transport from the airport but if you are held up or the plane arrives late, be adaptable. Remember – you're here now. Stretch, shake away the long journey and practise thinking positive.

GETTING TO KNOW YOURSELF IN JAPAN

You are in a non-English speaking country with plenty of new and unusual choices before you. What kind of person would you like to be? It's easy to get stressed on holiday but with a little bit of mind preparation before you go, you'll be able to glide through those normally stressful events.

A great way to get to know yourself in Japan is by getting to know the locals. If you are a bit shy like us, then taking yourself out of your comfort zone and trying to talk to locals is a brilliant way to learn more about the area you are visiting and possibly make some new friends. If we go somewhere we love, we'll always try and ask staff or locals if there is anything else in the neighbourhood they would recommend. Japanese people are so friendly. We've had people walk us to their favourite cafe, buy us their favourite drink, share their bento box lunch – and the list goes on.

We always catch ourselves smiling and laughing a lot in Japan. We've come to know the more relaxed and inquisitive versions of ourselves, and we are sure you will get to know your Japan self on your mindful holiday too.

A HOLIDAY FROM YOURSELF

Michelle loves to use this expression: 'A holiday from yourself', whilst in Japan. Her Japan takes her away from a busy work schedule, and also a busy psychological schedule. She likes to feel home melting away as the plane takes off. No tech on the plane is a completely relaxing zone. Landing in Japan instantly imbues her with a unique mindset. Steve feels an adventurous spirit rising within him – possibilities are around every corner.

HOLIDAY SLEEP HYGIENE

Always have earplugs on hand. Hotel noise can disrupt your sleep and wreak havoc on your holiday. Jet lag and unfamiliar surroundings can leave you a little discombobulated when travelling. However, Japan is the perfect place to feel unfamiliar as there are many small comforts you can bring with you or purchase to make your holiday relaxing. We suggest these:

· Japanese incense wafting around your room each night will relax you and help you to find your inner calm. Incense and burners are available in temples and homeware stores and specialist incense stores.

· We love Japanese forest essential oils, especially hinoki and cypress. Find a sleep blend and a portable diffuser.

· We take a bath with essential oils each night before sleep. If you are lucky enough to stay in a ryokan (traditional Japanese inn) or a hotel with a communal bath, a night-time onsen will calm you and soothe your weary limbs.

A TECH-FREE HOLIDAY

Having a phone for maps, translating, emergencies, contacting hotels and checking schedules has made travelling in the 21st century much easier. It has also kept us all connected to life at home which has helped keep our mind cluttered with the worries of work and possible stresses relating to family and friends. A holiday should be all about quieting one's mind. The term 'getting away from it all' exists for a reason. A holiday is a circuit-breaker, it should be about new experiences and a change of pace and culture. Being completely connected to home stops us from looking around us, trying new things and deeply relaxing into the here and now.

HOW TO MANAGE A TECH-FREE HOLIDAY

· Before you leave, think about the amount of time each day you want to spend on your devices. This is a holiday after all, so every moment counts!
· Don't look at your devices before you go to sleep. You don't want to be worried about anything on a holiday!
· Turn the internet off your phone in the daytime and just use your phone as a camera.
· If you are travelling with a friend(s) or family, have one designated person using their phone with wi-fi in the daytime.
· Invest in a small, good-quality camera and use it instead of a phone camera.
· Set up an email reply letting work colleagues and friends know you will be away and not answering correspondence.
· Let friends know you will be out of range and not checking your phone all the time.
· Put a timer on your phone or laptop and designate an amount of time per day to answer emails or texts.

A LITTLE WORD ABOUT SOCIALS

Sharing photos of a trip is this century's equivalent of a slide night. It can be fun and interesting in small amounts, but a relentless outpouring of images will have your friends and followers switching off. Letting people know you are away can be tricky in terms of security at home. It can mean random people in your life or strangers on your socials get in touch wanting to meet up if they are holidaying in the same place. In some cases this may be lovely, however if you have been saving all your pennies for a dream break, you should stick to your original schedule – but it can become stressful to say no to meet-ups. Maybe set a time limit.

Instead of posting, take photos with your mind's eye. Let the things you see sear themselves on your soul and burn themselves in your memory. Remember, experience is every bit as important as keepsakes and pictures. They can exist in harmony together. It's important to put into perspective having a great trip versus the proof of having a great trip. Here are our tips:

· Selfie sticks are almost never okay. They intrude on other travellers' space and can ruin others' experiences and photos.
· On the plane on the way home save your best pics into a folder and upload one per day to your socials on your return.

SUSTAINABLE TRAVEL

There are so many small things you can do to make your trip a sustainable one. Responsible tourism not only helps you to uphold your personal ethics in Japan, it also helps local communities. Here are our tips:

· Consider buying some of your travel essentials second-hand, like a suitcase, backpack and travel wallet. You'll save money and reduce your retail footprint by creating less waste.
· Bins in Japan will always have icons of what to put in them, such as bottles and cans, combustibles, PET, plastic, paper and others.
· Walk, hire a bicycle or use public transport to lower your carbon footprint.
· Bring your own water bottle and reusable bags or containers.
· Eat leftovers for snacks and picnics.
· Buy food that can be stored for a few days.
· Pack light.
· Don't get your towels washed every day.
· Buy souvenirs from small makers.
· Buy from vintage temple markets.
· Buy local goods like cloth or stationery that you can make into presents when you get home.
· Eat seasonally and avoid big chain and international stores.
· Take your own shopping bags – don't use plastic bags.
· The Japan Rail (JR) Pass or other rail passes can save money and help you to use public transport, rather than taxis or Ubers.

While there is no direct translation for mindfulness in Japan, Japanese language has an array of beautiful words that float around the concept.

WABI-SABI 侘寂

Woven into the very fabric of Japanese life, wabi-sabi is not just accepting, but finding beauty in life's imperfections. It's a colour added to the palette of the everyday that exists as a whisper, a word that can't be seen, an idea that can be felt but not grasped. The melting of snow; the falling sakura (cherry blossom) petals at the end of Hanami (cherry blossom season); the decay of a piece of wood in a forest; the beauty of ageing; the longing for lost things; a broken plate. At its core, this beautiful philosophy is all about finding meaning in our ever-changing world. Accepting the light and the dark, always seeing the world as a movable, continuous adventure.

When we travel there is the preconceived idea of what our trip will look like. It is said that one-third of a trip is the excitement of planning, the idea of a new adventure. Wabi-sabi is a wonderful concept to hold with you when travelling as our carefully planned itineraries are almost never hiccup-free. Wabi-sabi can help you to embrace the changes in schedules, rogue weather events, delays and unexplained diversions. Turning itinerary changes and travel difficulties into positive experiences will enrich the experiences for you and those around you.

MA 間

Ma is a concept where the 'spaces between and around' become an important or even central aspect of the object, art, building or thing you are observing. Ma is one of our favourite Japanese words. The space in-between things, not a day or an hour, just a moment. A fragment or a tiny piece. Seeing something others miss. Discovering the true shape and meaning of something by seeing what it is that makes that thing take shape.

When you're travelling, use ma to discover the unexpected, to uncover new experiences in the seemingly commonplace, to see familiar things in a new light.

IKIGAI 生き甲斐

Ikigai is a concept we can all live by. Living a happy life and using your core beliefs to shape your purpose and direction. Finding the right path forward to psychological and/or artistic fulfilment. Reaching goals, achieving dreams and moving forward, knowing you have tried your hardest to live the life you want to live.

While travelling, apply these core directives to shape the kind of holiday you will have and to bring personal meaning to your experiences.

MONO NO AWARE 物の哀れ, もののあはれ

Mono no aware means the awareness of impermanence, which in turn leads to a deeper appreciation and understanding of passing things – and of life itself. It is also the cultivation and celebration of ephemera and the power imbued within objects. As a designer, Michelle tries to live by this phrase every day. She feels deeply for the collection of ephemera she holds dear. The careful placement of objects in her house and garden. That nature around her is transient. She has a deep acknowledgement of the seasons. The importance of friendships and connections. The understanding that life is a cycle and she thinks often of the enormity of what is around her.

After your travels, if you find yourself rolling a faded object around in your hands, dwelling on time passing or opportunities missed and it fills you with melancholy – let that feeling fill your heart with an understanding of how the power of the past is instilled in the present.

UKIYO 浮世

If there is one word to hold dear to you on your trip it's ukiyo. Living in the moment, not thinking of the past or the future – just being. Compartmentalising work, relationships and cares.

Try new things. Experience everything. This is the joy of travel.

ICHI-GO ICHI-E 一期一会

One moment, one time. Ichi-go ichi-e is a Zen phrase that meditates on the chance of an experience that will only happen once in a lifetime. Your experiences while travelling will stay with you, imprint on your psyche, change and shape you.

After your travels, you'll find yourself recalling moments and fragments. A bell will remind you of a temple stay, a waft of incense a sacred site you visited. A one-time encounter can foster a lifetime of recalled memories. You could be having a one-time event, so cherish it!

YŪGEN (幽玄)

Yūgen says that real beauty is in subtlety and suggestion. Profound, graceful emotions can be stirred up not through the obvious, but in the essence. The concept of yūgen permeates every part of Japanese culture.

· Patina
· Raked gardens
· Candle- and low-lit teahouses
· The religion of Teaism
· The beauty in small things
· Watching with wonderment at the changing seasons
· Cherishing small moments

To practise yūgen on a holiday to Japan is to operate on a deeper level. Less words, more inner thought. Drifting, not rushing.

F
O
O
D

A CUISINE ALMOST TOO PRETTY TO EAT

Chances are many of your usual favourite foods will not be on offer in Japan, so enjoy the break from routine and try all the new things. Each prefecture you visit will offer up its own proud selection of local delicacies. Be mindful of the local produce and eat according to the season and climate. Always ask for the recommended specials. 'Omakase' means 'chef's choice' and is a wonderful way to discover what the locals eat and to find new favourites.

DESSERT AND SWEETS

Changing with the seasons and replete with beauty, wagashi (Japanese sweets) are a study in proportion and subtlety. Delicate and refined, they sit quietly whilst their Western counterparts parade in the foreground.

With flavours like red bean, chestnut, green tea, yuzu and sweet potato, these perfectly formed jewels will have you contemplating new flavours, new textures and new intensity. Try yokan (red bean paste and 'agar agar' sweets), manju (sweet balls filled with bean paste), daifuku (soft mochi and bean paste), mochi (rice dough with sweet filling), dango (sweet rice balls on a stick), monaka (rice wafers filled with red bean paste), yatsuhashi (rice dough with sweet filling) and more.

You may take a while to divest yourself of your Western sweet tooth, but soon you'll be an expert in the different kinds of Japanese sweets, you'll have your own favourites, and you'll seek out old backstreet, rustic sweet shops and the bejewelled sweets counter in every department store.

GLUTEN-FREE FOOD

Gluten-free food is available in Japan but not readily. Always ask. Soy sauce contains gluten so it's not just wheat-based foods you'll need to avoid. Try edamame (young soybeans in their pod), onigiri (rice balls), shio (grilled meat and vegetables flavoured with shio/salt, not soy), plain rice, omelettes and egg dishes, sushi and sashimi without soy sauce, salads without a soy-based dressing, nasu dengaku (eggplant grilled over a fire with miso paste), crackers and senbei (rice cakes). Miso soup and soba noodles can be gluten-free, but you will need to ask.

VEGETARIAN FOOD

Vegetarian food can be difficult in Japan due to the prevalence of bonito (fish) in many flavourings, but it is becoming much easier to find. Vegetarian dishes with dairy include onigiri (vegetable or seaweed riceballs), tamagoyaki (omelettes), onsen eggs (from hot springs), boiled eggs, potato salad (check, it can sometimes contain ham), omelette sushi and tamago-sando (egg sandwich).

VEGAN FOOD

You'll need to do a bit of research and ask questions when it comes to scoping out the additives in the food you eat. Department stores have good selections of fresh vegetables, salads and rice bentos. Convenience stores have soy drinks and soy-based desserts, packaged edamame (young soybeans in their pod), sushi rolls with pickles, salads and more. Vegan foods include salads, nasu dengaku (grilled eggplant

UMAMI

Umami is an elevated taste and something hard to put into words. It's that extra kick in your ramen broth, the indescribably delicious lingering taste in that tofu soup. It's a deep taste, found in meats, aged cheeses, sauces, seafood pastes and seaweeds. Often called the fifth taste, it somehow manages to capture elements of all four.

LANGUAGE TIPS

Please
Onegaishimasu

Excuse me
Sumimasen

**Thank you
(at the end of a meal)**
Domo arigatō gozaimashita

Can I have the bill please?
O kanjō onegaishimasu *or*
O kaikei onegaishimasu

At the start of the meal
Put your hands in prayer
position and say 'Itadakimasu',
which literally translates to
'I humbly receive'.

**At the end of a meal please
say this to your waiter and as
you are leaving**
Gochisousama deshita, which
translates as 'thank you for
the meal, it was
delicious/a feast'.

and miso), vegan ramen, Japanese sweets (manju, mochi and yokan), edamame, soy-based soft-serve ice-creams, pickles, soba or udon with dipping sauce on the side (make sure it doesn't include bonito), yuba (tofu skin) and hiyayakko (chilled tofu) but ask for all tofu without bonito flakes.

SHOJIN RYORI

This Buddhist cuisine, served at temples during your stay or if you visit for lunch, is like kaiseki ryori (Japanese cuisine course restaurants) in that it is a series of small dishes but it is much more rustic, nearly always plant-based, sourced from local ingredients and served on modest tableware. The monk's meal, shojin ryori is simple, light and plain, yet delicious, hearty and even elegant, having been perfected over centuries as a way to deeply enjoy food – despite a strict dietary regimen. Essential components are miso soup, tofu, soy, rice and mountain vegetables. If you have allergies, or follow a strict plant-based diet, ask the host – shojin ryori can easily accommodate.

TEA AND TEAISM

With its roots in China as a medicinal drink, the art of tea has evolved into a religious and spiritual experience in Japan. A cup of steeped leaves or whisked powder can evoke strong feelings. Drinking tea can be a time to rest and reflect, take stock and simplify. Tea will often be served to you when you sit down to eat, on arrival at a ryokan (traditional Japanese inn), after dinner at a restaurant, or in a teahouse or cafe with wagashi (Japanese sweets). It can be drunk hot or cold, is packed with antioxidants and is both an everyday drink and an elevated, high-end experience. Taking tea in a traditional or contemporary teahouse is always one of the highlights of our trip. There are many experiences to be had and you can find some of our favourites in our tea chapter (*see* p. 39).

KAISEKI RYORI

An exquisite feast of small dishes, each expertly prepared and served on notable ceramics and tableware, kaiseki ryori (*see* p. 96) is a harmonious balance of flavour, colour, texture and sight. It can be ordered in select restaurants or at ryokan guest houses. Although some dishes will be familiar with each meal, every kaiseki will be a different and memorable experience for the diner, bearing the signature dishes and style of the chef. Note the presentation – your carrot may have taken an hour to sculpt. A mindful trip in Japan would not be complete without experiencing kaiseki ryori.

SELF-CARE GIFTS TO BRING HOME

· Yukata (summer cotton kimono)
· Green tea (matcha, sencha, hojicha)
· Chawan (tea cup/bowl)
· Wooden facial and hand pressure-point massage tools
· Kintsugi (the art of visible repair) kit
· Zabuton (meditation cushion)
· Washi and origami paper
· Onsen (hot springs) bath salts
· Handmade objects from small makers
· Rice bran candles to light your room and to cast your own shadows
· Lacquer or wooden chopsticks
· Ceramics from local markets and makers
· Hydrating face masks
· Geta (wooden clogs) and zōri (sandals)
· Furoshiki (cloth wrapping)
· Bento boxes
· Paper and cloth fans

禅
道

The way
of Zen

MINDFUL TIP

The suffixes 'ji' and 'dera' mean 'temple'.

In 1938 when D.T. Suzuki penned *Zen Buddhism and Its Influence on Japanese Culture*, Zen was introduced to the Western world. Since then, Zen has been sitting in the lotus position at the very pinnacle of the concept of mindfulness. Based on the ancient Chinese 'Channa', a Buddhist doctrine which promotes an understanding of the body and mind through intense meditation and reflection, Zen teaches us to live perfectly in an imperfect world.

There are three distinct sects of Zen. The Obaku sect still chant their sutras in Chinese. The Rinzai sect was favoured by samurai and places emphasis on seated meditation and 'Koan', enigmatic sentences that promote thought ('just what IS the sound of one hand clapping ...?'). The Soto sect was originally practiced by the lower class, artisans, creatives and poets. The principal practise is zazen (meditation), which is performed in front of a blank space – like a curtain or wall.

Mindfulness and Zen are inextricably linked. Both promote ritual as a way to focus on the physical world, which in turn leads to self-discovery and a new perception of the true nature of being and your surroundings. The acceptance of suffering or difficulty in turn leads to the search for inner strength. Living a Zen life includes focusing on attainment of goals, healthy and restrained eating, an emphasis on kindness, improving the lives of others and a rigorous study of spiritual doctrines. Various methods are used to understand, enhance and attain Zen, including breathing, silence, contemplation, chanting mantras and the discipline of the martial arts. We have shared many of the traditional Japanese artisan crafts in this book from calligraphy (*see* p. 83) to painting and poetry, ikebana (*see* p. 84) and the tea ceremony (*see* p. 39), all of which have roots in Zen practice and promote patience, diligence and levels of achievement.

On your visit to Japan, you can participate in Zen practices, especially if you are staying at a temple (*see* p. 133) or visiting the ancient city of Kyoto. Zen zazen (meditation) classes are a perfect introduction. You'll find yourself in a beautiful temple hall sitting in the lotus position and clearing your mind of all clutter, so that beneficial thoughts and creative ideas can form in the newly created spaces. Visiting a Zen garden connects you with the thoughts and philosophies of the garden's creator. Add your newly acquired Zen philosophy to your own life, when driving in your car around the big city, at awkward family get-togethers or in stressful situations. Michelle always gets a carpark with her Zen parking philosophy.

Previous: Ginkakuji Temple; *opposite top left and bottom:* Nanzenji Temple; *opposite top right:* Ryoanji Temple

西芳寺

SAIHOJI (KOKEDERA) TEMPLE
KYOTO

56 Matsuo, Jingatanicho,
Nishikyo-cho, Kyoto

There are a few ways to get
there; we took bus 73 from
Kyoto station to Kokedera
Suzumushidera stop, then
walk (3min)

One of our most-treasured Zen gardens lies on the outskirts of western Kyoto.
Saihoji or, as it's affectionately known, Kokedera (moss temple), is a Rinzai Zen
temple with a magical moss garden. Dating back over 1200 years, the temple
is often thought of as a style template for many later Zen structures in Kyoto,
notably nearby Kinkakuji temple and Ginkakuji temple.

The beauty of the garden is so revered that some commitment to visiting is
required. Bookings are taken two months in advance, applying directly to the
monks by way of an approved postcard (online booking will be available in future).
We had our postcard denied twice before finally receiving an entry pass (nothing
personal – our desired dates were full). Kokedera understandably limit visitors to
keep their moss garden in pristine condition.

On our allotted day we entered the temple and were ushered into the hondo
(main hall) where we sat on the red carpeted floor at a Japanese desk and set
about inking our own Sutra onto wooden plaques before being allowed into the
garden. We followed the wonky path around the lake (ougonchi), which is shaped
like the Japanese character for 'heart' (shin). Over one hundred types of moss
blanket the ground, covering objects, rocks and scattered stones in soft grassy
cloaks. The moss gathers thickly around tree trunks and in smatterings on the
tiles of the temple roof. The central moss island with connecting stone bridges,
reflected in the mirror-still lake, is otherworldly and conjures thoughts of fairytale
worlds. The garden has a quiet feeling of melancholy, its cushiony patina growing
and changing over time.

A few notable scenes inhabit the grounds. The karesansui, a type of garden
shaped using only rock and stone, is a rare example of Zen principles. The
Shonantei teahouse has a moon-viewing platform, and a circular window frames
a mossy vista.

Saihoji is a great reminder of how nature can be your own place of worship,
or a perfect quiet space for meditation.

南禅寺

8-6 Nanzenji, Fukuchi-cho,
Sakyo-ku, Kyoto

Keage station, then walk
(10min)

NANZENJI TEMPLE
KYOTO

Nanzenji's quiet beauty is a must-visit for Zen travellers. Depending on where your journey is taking you, Nanzenji temple lies at the start or end of the Philosopher's Path. It's our Christmas day pilgrimage, a cherished part of our Japan, a sprawling complex with a collection of spectacular moments both visible and tucked away.

Part of the Rinzai sect and dating to the mid-13th century, Nanzenji is a living Zen museum. Its historical tapestry includes wars, invasions (the Tendai sect monks from Mount Hiei, unimpressed with the growing popularity of Zen practice, destroyed the temple in 1393 CE) and fires. We love the walk to the impressive Sanmon (mountain gate), built in 1628 CE, whose thick wooden pillars frame Nanzenji's hondo (main hall), surrounded by impressive autumn colours or thick carpets of moss.

Sub-temple Tenjuan's garden is one of Japan's hidden delights. The central pond garden featuring moss, bridges, waterfalls and rock formations is perfect for a contemplative stroll. You'll find us here in winter at dusk when the bells are ringing.

A rare and often overlooked treasure at Nanzenji is the hondo's Zen dry garden, commonly attributed to Kobori Enshu, one of the most famous Zen gardeners in Japan's history. The garden epitomises the central idea of tigers and cubs (represented by three large rocks and three small rocks) crossing through a stream (the white sand), which has become a popular dry garden theme across the country.

建仁寺

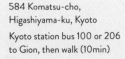

584 Komatsu-cho,
Higashiyama-ku, Kyoto

Kyoto station bus 100 or 206
to Gion, then walk (10min)

KENNINJI TEMPLE
KYOTO

With a story stretching back to 1202 CE, Kyoto's oldest Zen temple, Kenninji, is one of the Kyoto Gozan, the five most important Rinzai Zen temples in Japan. Founding priest Yosai was highly influenced by Zen in China and brought its teachings home with him. He is also known as the founder of the way of tea (*see* p. 39), which is as revered today as it was centuries ago.

Kenninji is just a short walk from the popular Gion district – easily accessed by Kyoto explorers. Treasures here include screens by Rinpa artist Sotatsu, depicting the gods of wind and thunder. Two favourite gardens of ours are here, the 'Garden of the Sound of the Tide' and the 'Circle, Triangle, Square' garden which represents the shapes which make up every aspect of the universe. The Dharma Hall dates back to 1765. An impressive work by Koizumi Jinsaku, *Twin Dragons* (2002), an ink on paper which celebrates the 800th anniversary of Kenninji, adorns the ceiling of the Hatto (lecture hall). The beautiful grounds include a must-see dry garden and many impressive buildings set against trees surrounded by thick mossy ground.

Kenninji offer classes including calligraphy and zazen (sitting meditation) under the instruction of Keinin Magami, the Deputy Head Monk of the temple. The same methods are used as those taught at the temple, including the Keisaku Zen stick, which uses posture and stability to bring body and mind into harmonious balance. Check online (kenninji.jp) for details.

仁和寺

NINNAJI TEMPLE
KYOTO

33 Omuroouchi, Ukyo-ku,
Kyoto
ninnaji.jp
Omuro Ninnaji station

Northern Kyoto is home to the sublime Ninnaji, a UNESCO World Heritage
Site. We return here often to walk the connecting wooden pathways, particularly
beautiful in the late afternoon, and languish in the gardens, gazing upon the two
historic tearooms: Hito-tei and Ryokaku-tei.

Head temple of the Shingon sect Omuro School, which highly regards physical
expressions of devotion, like prayers, rituals and chants, Ninnaji was founded in
888 CE. None of the original buildings remain, but the main hall, front gate,
inner gate and notable five-tiered pagoda date back to the early 1600s. Ninnaji is
famous as a viewing spot for sakura (cherry blossoms) but is one of the last temple
complexes to bloom, so it's a good place for an end-of-season immersive stroll
among the blushing pink. Popular Somei Yoshino blossoms adorn the main hall
and weeping cherry trees gird the bell tower in garlands of vibrant pink.

For hikers or strollers, Ninnaji has its own special mini version of the Shikoku
Henro (88 Temple Pilgrimage, *see* p. 190). The Omuro Pilgrimage begins behind
the temple. Its two-hour walking time takes in resplendent scenery.

Their five-guest shukubo (temple lodging) offers a luxurious and bespoke
experience for anyone who wants an unforgettable lifetime experience. Your
home for the night is a self-contained traditional house, your own tearoom and
dry garden. When the temple shuts its doors for the day, you'll be able to wander
the grounds as if the temple was your own home.

東福寺

15-778 Honmachi
Higashiyama-ku, Kyoto
tofukuji.jp
Tofukuji station, then
walk (10min)

TOFUKUJI TEMPLE
KYOTO

With a history stretching back to 1236 CE, Tofukuji sits in the head temple grounds of the Rinzai sect – one of Kyoto's most elegant spiritual compounds. The Sanmon gate is the oldest Zen gate in the world, dating back to 1425 CE. Kamakura-period (1192 to 1333) regent Kujo Michiie desired to build a temple in the image of the great Nara-period (794 to 1185 CE) complexes. Despite fires, war and the ravages of time, the magnificent buildings on the Tofukuji temple grounds still exude an ancient magic. Three bridges span the valleys along the way to the Kaisando, and in autumn the surrounding trees are aglow with blazing ochre and vermilion leaves.

Tofukuji boasts four unique gardens. Zen gardens are usually a solo feature on one side of the hojo (abbot's quarters). At Tofukuji the Zen gardens surround the hall. Famed gardener and historian Mirei Shigemori designed the gardens in 1939 and drew on his education in Nihonga painting, ikebana and the tea ceremony to create gardens which were unafraid to include major Western influences. Today it feels like it could have been designed centuries ago, yesterday or tomorrow.

Our favourite, the north garden, features a checkerboard of randomly placed squares which punctuate a fluffy carpet of grass edged with domed hedges. Walk around and observe the differences in the four gardens. For a Zen garden experience, it's one of a kind.

龍安寺

13 Ryoanji
Goryonoshita-cho,
Ukyo-ku, Kyoto

ryoanji.jp

Ryoanji station,
then walk (7min)

RYOANJI TEMPLE
KYOTO

The 'Temple of the Dragon at Peace' and UNESCO World Heritage Site Ryoanji is home to the best-known dry garden in Japan. The garden is said to contain four secrets or mysteries, left to the viewer to experience and then decipher, so take up a position on the wooden temple walkway and meditate deeply upon the garden and its significance.

Our first visit was in autumn on a cold Kyoto morning. We entered the main gate, circled the expansive pond, then walked the pilgrims path to the hojo (abbot's quarters, 1450 CE). We admired the beautiful painted sliding doors, then found ourselves before the dry garden. Whilst most sit on the wooden floor of the hojo to view the garden, we had read that in order to view all the stones one must stand. We focused our eyes firstly on the earthen coloured walls that framed a rectangle of perfectly raked sand. Rocks jutted out of the sand, meticulously placed by the designer, some sitting on their own mossy islands.

The meaning of the garden, thought to be as simple as the standard island or tiger and cub motif, or a complex secret of deep historical significance, has been the subject of much discussion between students of Zen Buddhism and the public alike. Some believe the garden represents infinity – a commonly held theory. It is widely agreed upon, however, that the garden's meaning, like its origin, is a mystery. The garden designer's identity has been misplaced through history, thus adding a deeper layer to the story.

On further exploration of the grounds, we admired the tearoom and Wabisuke Tsubaki, Japan's oldest camellia tree. We purified our hands in the stone water basin before lunching at their specialty tofu restaurant, Yudofu Umegaean, which has stunning views onto a mossy garden.

銀閣寺

GINKAKUJI TEMPLE
KYOTO

2 Ginkakuji-cho, Sakyo-ku
Kyoto

shokoku-ji.jp/en/ginkakuji

Bus 5, 17 or 100 from Kyoto
station to Ginkakuji-michi bus
stop, then walk (3min)

A peaceful stroll alongside the moss-adorned canal of the Philosopher's Path
will find you in good company. The great Japanese thinker Nishida Kitaro walked
along the path during his meditations, his antennae primed to receive inspiration.
Crowds may block your transmission in cherry blossom season, so tread the path
in the early morning or at fading light.

Ginkakuji, the silver temple, sits at the northern end of the Philosopher's Path
(Nanzenji, *see* p. 26, sits at the southern end). Dating back to 1482 CE, the
retirement villa of Shogun Ashikaga Yoshimasa was meant to be silver plated,
but sadly he ran out of funds. The temple is now known for its beautiful gardens,
breathtaking views over Kyoto (from the top of the garden path) and the rather
unique dry garden made of sand. The dry garden comes complete with one of
Ginkakuji's most curious objects, a giant sand cone, the kogetsudai or 'moon-
viewing platform'. It is said that it resembles the moon's reflection in a still pond if
observed from the top floor of the temple. Leading up to the platform the sand
looks like a simple striped path, however on further contemplation it is made up
of a subtly beautiful pattern, intricate and painstakingly complex in execution.

The mountainous setting calms you as do the manicured trees and walkways.
We first visited in deep winter and the dry garden was covered in a thin blanket
of snow. We were reminded of the Zen proverb ... no snowflake ever falls in the
wrong place ...

大雄山最乗寺

DAIYUZAN SAIJOJI TEMPLE
HAKONE

1157 Daiyucho,
Minami Ashigara
Kanagawa
Wakayama prefecture

daiyuuzan.or.jp

Daiyuzan station, then
bus or walk (45min)

A couple of hours from Tokyo you'll find yourself off the tourist grid, relaxing in quiet nature and being at one with Zen's rich history. Saijoji, hidden in the lush, mountainous forests north-east of Hakone, dates back to 1394 CE and its legacy has seeped into every tree, flower and building on the expansive grounds. A major power spot, the temple's benefits are many. We immersed ourselves in the abundant vegetation and ancient cedars that bejewel the inner spaces of the temple sanctum. The blazing glory of the autumn leaves offsets the dark of the temple buildings with splashes of vibrant colour.

We absorbed ourselves in morning and evening prayers at the Goshinden (worship hall) before strolling through Gekkai-mon gate and over Gokku-bashi (a beautiful bridge with a view of distant Sanshin-no-taki waterfall). Beautiful Okunoin shrine greeted us after we ascended the 354 stone steps that reach the highest point of the Daiyu mountain. We drank the 'diamond water' from the Kongousuidou spring, which is said to heal disease. Searching the grounds for the famed holy animals, we found carvings of the ryu (dragon), ikkakuju (unicorn) and komainu (guardian dog), all who are imbued with various powers (the ikkakuju, for instance, will cure you of disease and bless you with a pregnancy if you touch it ...).

Saijoji is a deeply religious experience ensconced in nature, where the power of Zen exists in everything around you. Take some of the stillness home with you to help you find the quiet in loud places.

宝徳寺

5-1608 Kawauchi-cho,
Kiryu, Gunma

visit-gunma.jp/en/spots/
hotokuji-temple

Kiryu station north exit,
then bus (25min)

HOTOKUJI TEMPLE
KIRYU

Hotokuji, a Rinzai sect Buddhist temple, dates to circa 1450 CE. Hotokuji is also called Koyo (changing autumn colours), as it famously shines in autumn when it plays host to one of our favourite Zen experiences.

During November, people flock to the temple to see the beautiful reds and yellows of momiji (autumn foliage), reflected in the highly polished floors (yuka) of the Zen-style main hall. Stretching out before the trees like a mirror-still lake, the floor creates a new world, a fantastical dimension of blazing autumn trees. There are some 100 trees on the temple grounds that are mirrored in the gleaming floor. Remove your shoes, assume the lotus position, and meditate upon the new consciousness created by the leaves, where everything is ruled by the potent beauty and transitory nature of life, a perfect summation of the concept of wabi-sabi. The floor is also spectacular in the snowy winter, or when the autumn trees are illuminated at dusk or during summer greenery.

An unmissable Zen manicured rock garden sits in front of the main hall and can be observed through a large katomado (flower window). It is said that the rock garden spiritually complements the changing colours of the autumn leaves.

MINDFUL TIP

You can't walk on the polished floors, you must gaze out onto them from another room.

鈴木大拙館

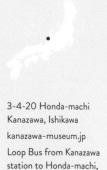

3-4-20 Honda-machi
Kanazawa, Ishikawa

kanazawa-museum.jp

Loop Bus from Kanazawa
station to Honda-machi,
then walk (4min)

D.T. SUZUKI MUSEUM

KANAZAWA

D.T. Suzuki (The D in D.T. stands for Daisetzu, meaning 'great humility', a
name conferred upon him by his Zen master) was a Zen scholar and writer in
the early 20th century. As a translator, writer and philosophy professor in Tokyo,
London and America (not to mention Zen student at Kamakura's Engakuji),
Suzuki was pivotal in the introduction of Zen principles to a Western audience.
Mindful travellers will find a spiritual home at the D.T. Suzuki Museum, a quiet
contemplative space devoted to Suzuki's theories of Zen built in Kanazawa's
Honda-machi, Suzuki's birthplace.

As he was considered a Zen Modernist, the museum's design is a perfect
reflection of Suzuki's work. Peruse his writings, photographs, books and
important cultural objects in the English-friendly exhibition spaces, before
heading out into the spiritual courtyard. The minimalist structure is stripped of
all decoration, its simplicity a form of intimacy. A white box, reached by a short
platform, is surrounded by a mirror-like pool of water which comes up to the
very edges of the walkway. The box is a contemplation room which invites you to
gaze up into the heavens or out into the still water. Architect Yoshio Taniguchi,
whose CV is as dense as Suzuki's (he designed MOMA in New York), has, we
think, designed a building which appears to be in a constant state of meditation
and repose.

The museum challenges you to become one with the building and experience
Zen in an organic way. Across the water is a one-person platform, like a jetty to
infinity. We stood at the water's very edge, gazing into the glassy surface, a spout
bubbling up at timed intervals, ripples spreading out like new ideas.

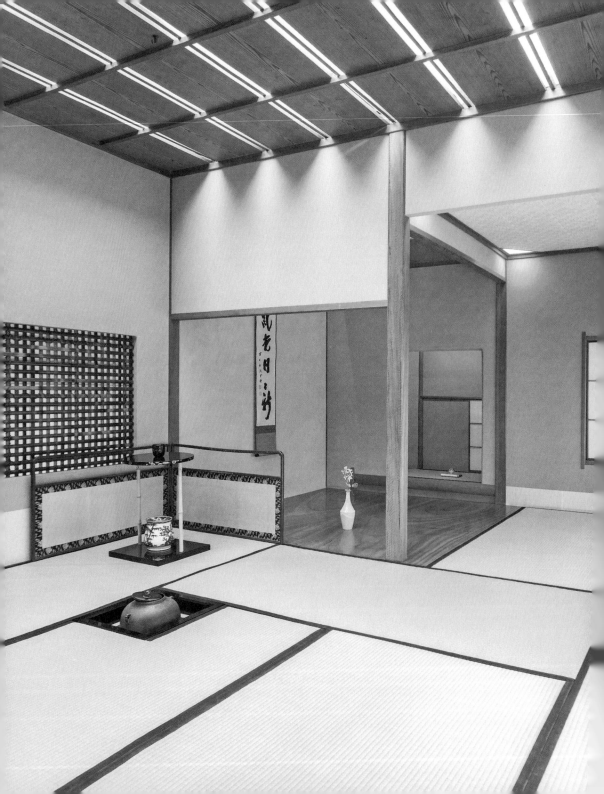

茶道

The way of tea

Chado (the tea ceremony, or the way of tea), along with Kodo (the way of incense, *see* p. 80), and Kado (the way of flowers, *see* p. 84), are considered the three classical refined arts in Japan. The earliest records of tea or cha 茶 in Japan date back to the 8th century CE when tea was introduced from China. However, it wasn't until the 16th century when, using the principles of wabi-sabi, early pioneers of the tea ceremony, Zen Buddhist monks Murata Jukō and Sen no Rikyū, gave it spiritual status. Using the doctrine of wabi-sabi, tea was no longer a luxurious extravagance, but a humble ceremony using minimalist ikebana displays and unadorned ceramics in natural colours.

The architecture of a chashitsu (teahouse) is a lesson in simplicity. How you enter, the position you sit in and the view – all are considered. During the ceremony, the water is boiled to the precise temperature and the chawan (matcha bowl) you are designated is carefully chosen. Contemplative silence is broken by the sound of the whisk stirring the matcha powder into the tea. Artful wagashi (Japanese sweets) complement the ritual. You enter a trance-like state and emerge at the end feeling revived and refreshed, physically and spiritually.

Historically, tea was once only for nobles, but was quickly adopted by the people. As Okakura Kakuzo observes in *The Book of Tea* (1906): 'It (tea) has permeated the elegance of noble boudoirs and entered the abode of the humble'. The teahouse's nijiri-guchi (crawl-in space) made all people bow when entering. The wealthy would have to divest themselves of finery and samurai remove armour and swords.

Japanese tea comes in various forms including matcha, the slightly bitter green powder ground from leaves, most often used in the tea ceremony; sencha, steeped matcha leaves; hojicha, leaves roasted in porcelain over charcoal; and genmaicha, a blend of roasted popped rice and green tea leaves.

Tea has become an essential part of our travel while in Japan. It presses pause on the day, giving us space to reflect and relax. Japanese tea will be served in many of the places you will visit, eat or stay, and is an important way for a host to share their kindness with you. However you take your tea, focus on the joy of it. Concentrate on the way your hands feel around the ceramic bowl; shut your eyes and feel the steam swirl about you; take in the pure scent of the steeped leaves wafting in the air; enjoy the deep, frothy green of the whisked matcha, or the refreshing jolt of a cold tea in high summer or a soul-warming sencha in winter.

Tea enthusiasts should head to Fuji City in Shizuoka in late April and May when the rows of tea hedges are at their most plump before the leaves are picked. At Obuchi Sasaba and Imamiya, a snow-capped Mount Fuji acts as an impressive backdrop to the expansive grids of billowy, tubular hedges. From the teahouses in gardens and temples and quiet ceremonies in beautiful rooms to the sprawling tea fields in Uji (see pp. 46 and 48), Kagoshima and Shizuoka, tea is infused into the very history of Japan. It is ritual, poetry and art. In the end, however, it's all about taking time out to enjoy the perfect brew.

Previous: Tokoan at Imperial Hotel; opposite top left: Tea fields at Obuchi Sasaba, Shizuoka; opposite top right: Tea and sweets in Uji; opposite bottom: Steve drinking matcha at Taizoin Temple

丸久小山園　西洞院店

561 Sanbonishitoin-cho,
Nakagyo-ku, Kyoto
marukyu-koyamaen.co.jp
Kurasuma Oike station exit 4-1

NISHINOTOIN TEA SHOP AND MOTOAN TEAHOUSE
KYOTO

Marukyu Koyamaen tea company's founder Kyujiro Koyama started honing his tea-making skills in Uji in the Edo period (1603 to 1867). Today, his family revere their ancestor's deep-rooted traditions whilst bringing the tea-making process into the 21st century. Their expansive estate of tea fields grows and manufactures tea sold in their tea shops and in in-house stores in the chic departments stores of Takashimaya and Isetan in Kyoto.

Marukyu Koyamaen's shop in Kyoto's south-west, Nishinotoin, is a beautiful machiya (traditional wooden townhouse) with a dark wooden façade, noren curtains and low-lit paper lanterns. Join the elegant clientele in a chic room with ikebana, a hanging scroll and floor-to-ceiling windows overlooking a courtyard garden. Nishinotoin Tea Shop is one of the finest establishments in Japan and their motto, 'Making teas with quality as the highest priority', is reflected in every part of the store and merchandise. Available for purchase are both high-end ceremonial-grade matcha and cooking-grade matcha, in stylish canisters perfect to display at home or as a gift for that design-obsessed friend.

Their teahouse, Motoan, serves Marukyu Koyamaen's premium tea in their chado (way of tea) experience. A separate sweets menu includes matcha and hojicha ice-cream and kakigori (shaved-ice desserts) in summer, but it's hard to go past the matcha roll cake, baumkuchen infused with subtle tea flavours with an irresistible dark green gooey centre. A traditional chashitsu (teahouse) is re-created on the grounds, complete with a nijiri-guchi (crawl-in space).

Don't leave without purchasing a matcha whisk and original tea-ware to practise your tea-making skills at home. Check online (marukyu-koyamaen.co.jp) for availability of their excellent workshops on how to prepare a bowl of matcha.

一保堂

52 Teramachi dori,
Tokiwagi-cho,
Nakagyo-ku, Kyoto

ippodo-tea.co.jp

Shiyakusho-mae station exit 11,
then walk (5min)

IPPODO TEA
KYOTO

Three centuries of selling tea 'blessed by mother nature' and picked in the fertile local tea fields has made Ippodo one of Japan's most respected and memorable teahouses. It's the quintessential Kyoto tea-shopping experience, from the elegant dark wooden exterior with the iconic Kanji logo splashed over white noren (traditional fabric curtains) to the vaulted dark wood-beam ceiling and the staff's immaculate uniforms and flawless service.

The tea varieties are extensive, with sencha, matcha, hojicha and genmaicha all available to buy in Ippodo's iconic tins. Visit the cafe where tea comes in a set with seasonal sweets. If you choose a sencha or bancha it will arrive with a small teapot, three teacups and a timer. Phrases like 'tea leaves unravelling' and 'do not agitate' will be lightly mentioned. If you're curious about which teas are shade or open-field cultivated, book in for a tea class or tasting session.

At Christmas, line up for their limited edition, early leaf New Year's tea, a tradition of ours every time we spend Christmas in Kyoto. Ippodo also sells teapots, whisks, cups and canisters which are some of the most precious gifts and keepsakes to take home that you'll find in Japan.

高台寺

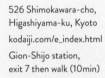

526 Shimokawara-cho,
Higashiyama-ku, Kyoto

kodaiji.com/e_index.html

Gion-Shijo station,
exit 7 then walk (10min)

TEA CEREMONY AT KODAIJI TEMPLE
KYOTO

A sidestep from popular Gion Dori, Kodaiji is a small Rinzai sect Buddhist temple which dates back over 400 years. Its theme is lacquer and gold – the embellished surface of the original temple – and anyone inspired by the melding of these two luxurious elements should not miss the shrine of Toyotomi Hideyoshi (his remains are interred in the Otamaya). The Kangetsudai (moon-viewing platform), Omotetmon (Gate to Sanctuary), canopied bridges and impressive sakura (cherry blossom) and maple trees all conspire to make Kodaiji one of Kyoto's most tranquil and atmospheric temples.

If you want to see a traditional chashitsu (teahouse), there are three on the grounds. On our first visit we admired the architecture of Ihoan (cottage of lingering fragrance). As one of Japan's best examples of a 16th-century chashitsu, with an oversized thatched roof sprouting over slightly ramshackle yellow walls, accented by large latticed windows, it is a sight to behold. Tea master Sen-no-Rikyu designed the chashitsu, imbuing it with all the elements of his concept of wabi-cha (beautiful, simple tea).

There are eight different tea ceremonies held at various times, dates and places around the temple grounds. For our second visit we booked ahead by phone (75-561-9966) for the morning tea ceremony. Held once a day, for an hour, with only three participants, it begins with a primer on the history of tea and tea customs, manners and ceramics before presenting an intimate, traditional ceremony. It is held in Japanese, but an English translator is provided for non-Japanese groups.

対鳳庵

Togawa-2, Uji, Kyoto
city.uji.kyoto.jp
Uji station (Nara line),
south exit, then walk (20min)

TAIHOAN
UJI

A side-trip from Kyoto, the historic town of Uji is the spiritual home of tea. The streets of Omotesando-dori are lined with stores selling a staggering array of matcha (green tea) varieties, teapots, utensils and ceramics. All manner of food including noodles and curries are matcha flavoured, and matcha dessert and soft serve ice-cream shops and cafes have queues around the block.

Taihoan is an unadorned, atmospheric sukiya-zukuri style teahouse. The name means 'teahouse across from the phoenix', as it's in a direct line (as the phoenix flies) from the golden bird that sits atop the impressive Ho-o-do (main hall) in the adjacent Byodoin temple grounds. Taihoan is run by the city of Uji and offers a tea ceremony prepared by Tea Ceremony Association members in traditional dress.

Drop-in guests can spend 30 minutes enjoying Light Tea – a perfectly whisked bowl of matcha and wagashi (Japanese sweets), although we highly recommend reserving in advance for the 50-minute Dark Tea/Light Tea set. The dark brew uses three times as much tea as a usual bowl of matcha and has a richer flavour. It also comes with a classic bowl of whisked matcha (the light tea) and wagashi. For an extra fee you can learn from the masters in the 40-minute Otemae (etiquette of tea ceremony) experience performed in the Ritsurei room. The otemae provides you with your own guide who will take you through the careful steps of performing a tea ceremony.

中村藤吉本店 宇治本店

NAKAMURA TOKICHI HONTEN
UJI

10 Ichiban, Uji
Uji City, Kyoto
tokichi.jp
Uji station (Nara line)
south exit, then walk (5min)

Waft out of Uji station and follow the scent of brewing tea. Before long you will arrive at the beautiful exterior of Nakamura Tokichi's head store, established in 1854. Float through the hemp noren curtains emblazoned with the famed Nakamura logo and you'll find yourself in a Garden of Eden for tea lovers. The beautiful space is a designated Important Cultural Landscape, as well as a hugely popular tea and sweets destination.

Prepare to queue for the cafe. The sweets include towering parfaits emblazoned with the Nakamura Tokichi logo, brimming with matcha sponge, jelly, mochi and ice-cream. Tea-infused kakigori (shaved-ice desserts), matcha sponge trifles, roll cake, and ice-cream with red bean paste are just some of the temptations on offer. We perused the extensive list of teas, ranging from delicate to adventurous. Nakamura have a special seven types blend using the Japanese process of gogumi: blending tea to get a perfect balance. The sencha is made unshaded, giving it a more bitter taste (Nakamura are proud of the fact that their sencha is traditional, despite many tea farms taking out the bitterness to appease the modern palate).

Afterwards, we visited the bountiful and beautiful store to stock up on teas, utensils, roll cake and tea-infused chocolate. For something special, don't miss the tea ceremony or the hiki-cha (Ground Tea Experience) at Zuishoan, a rare and elegant Genroku-period (1688 to 1704) teahouse. You can either partake in a traditional ceremony or grind your own tea leaves with a stone mill to make matcha. Sessions take around 90 minutes and you should book online (tokichi.jp) at least one day in advance.

ワドゥ

WAD OMOTENASHI CAFE
OSAKA

Wad's small but perfectly formed tearoom is a highlight of every trip we take to Osaka. Finding the tiny sign and climbing the steep stairs is all part of the reveal of Wad's contemporary take on a traditional tea ceremony room. Inside, moss-filled terrariums hang before wafting noren curtains. Staff float around the room in immaculate linen uniforms. Low-hanging lights, warm woods and repurposed furniture give the room that special simple and rustic, yet precious, feel that the Japanese have perfected.

Omotenashi means hospitality, and your experience at Wad will be a masterclass in sophisticated subtlety. The menu is concise, a curated selection of tea from Wazuka-cho (Kyoto). Cold and hot matcha, sencha and hojicha are served as a set with wagashi (Japanese sweets). When you order the matcha, staff let you choose a handmade vessel before whisking the tea, so use your intuition and select the one that resonates with you. The kakigori (shaved-ice dessert) is a must (especially in summer), and we like to order it with red bean and syrup as extras. Wad also has a gallery curating their favourite artists from around the country and you can buy expertly chosen ceramics displayed in the tearoom. Wad is a local favourite, and worth queuing for. Once seated, your mind and body will be transported to a magical time and place – simply beautiful.

Toshin bldg 2F,
4-9-3 Minamisenba,
Chuo-ku, Osaka

wad-cafe.com

Shinsaibashi station exit 3

東光庵

1-1-1 Uchisawa-cho,
Chiyoda-ku, Tokyo

Yurakucho station,
then walk (5min)

TOKOAN AT IMPERIAL HOTEL
TOKYO

The grand, stately and decidedly luxe Imperial is one of Tokyo's most revered
hotels. Surprisingly, it features a beautiful traditional-style teahouse on the
fourth floor. The Tokoan tea ceremony space is no mere room, but a perfectly
realised re-creation of a traditional sukiya-zukuri style teahouse with a classic
three-chambered structure. Architectural excellence imbues it with a sense
of the contemporary, yet heading inside the tearoom from the Western-style
Imperial hotel is a bit of a shock, as it seems to be a room out of time and place –
and that is the intention. It is designed to take you out of the everyday and to a
more refined, sophisticated world, like that of a classical teahouse in the deep
countryside rather than in urban Tokyo.

Walk along the perfectly placed stones, letting the low lighting and subtle
atmosphere set the mood. Sit and meditate upon the space, with its various
chambers leading to anterooms, the musty-sweet smell of tatami rising up and
mingling with the heady aroma of tea. Your host, demonstrating the pinnacle of
chado (way of tea) omotenashi, the deep and open-hearted care of the guest, will
float delicately around the space, each subtle flick of the wrist and movement of
the hands divulging another part of the wonderful chado tea ceremony. Sit quietly
and partake of the delicious tea and seasonal sweets. It's a flawless tea ceremony
experience for those who are unable to venture out of the big city. Book in
advance online (imperialhotel.co.jp/e/tokyo/facility/tokoan).

MINDFUL TIP

Attention architect buffs:
Frank Lloyd Wright designed
the second incarnation of
Tokyo's Imperial Hotel. It was
designed in the Mayan
Revival style, opened in June
1923 and famously survived
the Great Kantō earthquake
in September 1923. It was
partly destoyed in World
War II and sadly
demolished in 1967.

櫻井焙茶研究所

SAKURAI JAPANESE TEA EXPERIENCE
TOKYO

Spiral bldg 5F, 5-6-23
Minami Aoyama,
Minato-ku, Tokyo

Omotesando station exit B1

After 14 years perfecting his craft, tea master Shinya Sakurai opened the teahouse Sakurai, where he presents a contemporary version of the traditional tea ceremony on the refurbished fifth floor of the Spiral building in the chic Omotesando area of Tokyo. An exceptional date venue or place to take your architecture- or design-obsessed friends, every part of the visually stunning tearoom is carefully crafted and considered, including the exquisite signage. The minimalist space is accented by brass and polished concrete. The glass sink is a notable feature, with a shimmering waterfall disappearing into its shallow bowl.

You will be shown to a counter seat by a square bench where the tea master will work his magic for all to see, whisking, agitating and pouring – tea making that commands silence. Hojicha is roasted in store and seasonal varieties are brewed using elaborate kettles and teapots and poured into elegant ceramics. Varieties are drawn from the best tea regions in Japan and blended to perfection before your very eyes. Enjoy your tea with some of Tokyo's most beautifully made seasonal wagashi (Japanese sweets) while you gaze out over the impressive skyline. Head to Sakurai as the sun sets for their excellent tea-infused cocktails.

如庵

1 Gomonsaki, Inuyama,
Aichi

Inuyama station, then
walk (15min)

JOAN AT URAKUEN GARDEN

INUYAMA

On a crisp autumn day, we made a pilgrimage to the 400-year-old teahouse
Joan inside Inuyama's Urakuen garden. Designed as a cha-niwa, a garden
made primarily for the tea ceremony, Urakuen is a fairytale stroll along moss-
covered paths, among windswept trees, bamboo groves, lanterns, wooden
gates and rooftops made of cypress – all particularly resplendent in autumn's
seasonal colours.

One of the three oldest and finest teahouses in Japan, Joan teahouse was built
in 1618 by Oda Uraku, a disciple of famed tea ceremony master Sen-no-Rikyu.
Originally situated in Kyoto, the teahouse was moved in 1972 and now sits happily
in the lush grounds of Urakuen.

Although you can no longer enjoy a tea ceremony here, Joan was designated
a National Treasure in 1951 and should be visited by tea devotees, students of
history or anyone fascinated with the wabi-sabi aspects of teahouse architecture.
Gaze upon it from the outside to feel the centuries of ceremony infused in
its walls. Note how the yellow exterior walls belie the warm, dark, mismatched
woods and delicate framing of the interior space. Observe the small nijiri-guchi
(crawl-in space) three-tatami-mat preparation area, separated by a one-and-a-
half-tatami-mat corridor. Peer though the simple yet effortlessly stylish lattice
bamboo window. Joan is the perfect example of the classic chashitsu (teahouse).

If Joan has given you a humble thirst for tea, we highly recommend nearby
Syodenin Shion, Oda Uraku's house in later life, which serves tea and wagashi
(Japanese sweets) using locally made ceramics.

懐華樓

1-14-8 Higashiyama,
Kanazawa, Ishikawa

Kanazawa Loop bus
to Hashiba-cho, then
walk (5min)

KAIKARO
KANAZAWA

An impressive site in Kanazawa's Higashi Chaya (East teahouse) district, Kaikaro, a geisha teahouse, exudes enchantment even before you have entered the building. The kimusuku (lattice wood windows) create an alluring interplay of shadow and light which falls gently on the cobbled street. At night it is at its most alluring, but the love is unrequited – you'll find you have a wistful longing to enter and partake in the geisha performances, but this is reserved for patrons and their 'referrals' only. On the scheduled occasions that a performance is open to the public (keep an eye on the website – kaikaro.jp), beg, borrow or steal tickets for an unforgettable experience.

During the day however, Kaikaro allows all of us a rare glimpse into an Edo-period (1603 to 1867) teahouse, dating back to 1820. Higashi Chaya is the largest Chaya in Kanazawa and proudly designated a Kanazawa City Architectural. Kaikaro is one of its most impressive teahouses and you can feel a real sense of history in Kaikaro's small hall where geisha perform and tea ceremonies are held. We particularly loved the striking vermilion lacquer stairs and the arresting fusuma paintings on the screen doors. The golden tearoom is a highlight, as is the curious mishmash of patterns and designs on walls, partitions and tatami mats. Head downstairs for tea and sweets. We were lucky enough to sit at the central table with a traditional open fire and hanging central kettle. Matcha was whisked with gold flecks as per the style in Kanazawa. It is a custom for geisha to gift paper fans to their clientele with their names on them, like elaborate calling cards, and Kaikaro offer guests the opportunity to write their own name on a paper fan using simple calligraphy. Classes are available throughout the day but require reservations online.

温泉道

The way of onsen

Discard both your clothes and daily cares and enjoy a time-honoured bathing ritual in one of Japan's 3000 hot springs. Onsen have been revered for centuries for their relaxing and healing qualities. We have visited over 250 onsen, from rural bathhouses to forest retreats and whole towns dedicated to taking a bath, as well as city purpose-built super sento (large bathing and relaxing centres). On each trip to Japan, we always stay in at least two ryokan (traditional Japanese inns) based on the beauty of their baths. This passion inspired us to pen *Onsen of Japan*, one of our favourite book-writing experiences.

Communal naked bathing can be a sacred ritual, a form of deep relaxation and a way to relieve ailments. It's not an exclusive day spa – it's an affordable, social experience, an outing where family or friends can enjoy each other's company and engage in 'hadaka no tsukiai', or 'naked communication'. Everyone is equal in the bath and conversations – deep or casual – can be had while in a relaxed state.

Preparing for an onsen is a precise ritual (*see* p. 60 for an express lesson). Putting your clothes in the locker, washing your body, then sinking into the hot springs and letting your mind drift away from clutter and cares is all part of the process. Apart from the relaxation, onsen water has a range of natural beneficial ingredients, including chlorides for healing burns and for easing joint and muscle pain; sulphur for bronchitis and blood pressure; iron for blood disorders; aluminium for dermatitis; and sodium bicarbonate and alkaline for impossibly soft skin.

Can there be anything more mindful than steeping in hot water, soaking and meditating while you gaze upon snow-kissed mountains, verdant forest glades or fields aglow with bright summer flowers? While the Western world obsesses over the work–life balance, Japan was always ahead of the curve and the onsen is the perfect 'wellness retreat' and, for us, absolute heaven. As an added bonus, most onsen and super sento will feature all the best health and wellbeing treatments, including relaxation rooms, saunas, massage, reflexology and more.

Previous: Tsuru No Yu; *opposite top left:* Hoshi Onsen Chojukan; *opposite top right:* Manhole cover at Kusatsu Onsen; *opposite bottom:* Onsen shoes lined up, ready to wear

THE ART OF THE ONSEN

HOW TO ONSEN

An onsen will be one of the most relaxing and mindful things you will do on your Japanese trip. Are you confident to tackle the bathhouse? Quite often there seems to be too many things to remember, too many rules, too many mistakes that can be made. But it can be quite simple, so try not to panic, be mindful of others and, most of all, expect to make a few mistakes. We share the following tips with you:

- Remove your shoes, put them in the lockers and slip into the sandals provided. These shoe lockers will usually be inside the building but outside the onsen changing room. There may be a fee or a refundable ¥100 deposit, and there will be a key, a block of wood (in older onsen) or piece of metal that slots into the lock.

- The attendant will show you the way to, or point to, the entrance to the onsen changeroom. This is usually through a noren curtain which is almost always pink or red for girls and blue for guys. The attendant may also give you a towel or onsen kit for an extra fee.

- Bathing can be tricky to navigate for people who are transgender or don't identify with the traditional gender binaries. Try mixed bathing or private bathing onsen facilities and check ahead for specific information.

- Inside the changeroom you'll see people standing around in various states of undress. You only need to take one thing into the actual bath with you and that's the small washcloth you are now using to self-consciously cover your private parts (you may also slip your locker key band over your wrist after placing your things in your locker).

- For anyone with shoulder-length or longer hair, please tie your hair up. Hair dangling in the water is considered bad manners.

- Now you are inside the bathhouse, find the rows of taps and bath bowls and claim one that is free. In a sento or onsen, this is the moment to sit down and take your time. Each cubicle has a stool and a bath bowl. Take your stool and give it a rinse then have a seat. Use the products to wash your whole body and then make sure you rinse thoroughly.

- When you enter the bathing area, you may be hit with a huge choice of bathing options. Many factors go towards choosing where to start. For instance, if the weather is warm, we start with the indoor baths and end with the outdoor baths. If we have sore muscles we may choose to try a jet bath, then end with a more relaxing bath. If the weather is cold we will spend all our time in the outside baths (there is nothing more beautiful than being outdoors in hot water while it is snowing). Hinoki cedar wood baths are rustic and special. Many baths have the temperature on the wall for you to see. Depending on the weather, you may decide not to enter the cold plunge bath in winter or the super-hot ones in summer.

- The smell of the water may be a factor for you. Choose a smell you like if the bathhouse has more than one water source or if it has a medicinal or seasonal bath.

- After the bath, wash again and then check out the mirrored grooming station in each onsen. Some will have blow-dryers, face creams, hair ties, cotton buds, brushes, hair oil, moisturiser, and in special cases products made locally from the onsen water. In general, the more you pay on entry to the bathhouse the more lavish this section is.

- Be sure to hydrate. Always have a drink before and after a bath. There should be a water fountain in the changeroom, and you can try a small yoghurt drink, coffee or chocolate milk (there will always be a vending machine in or around the changerooms). These mini pick-me-ups are a good way to both rehydrate and refuel after the hot water. We can't have a bath without having one of these drinks afterwards!
- Fruit is a great replenisher. We've seen mini fruit stalls set up out the front of bathhouses for this reason. Yoghurt drinks, green tea and, for many people, a local beer really hit the spot. Make sure to seek out and make use of the relaxation room if your bathhouse has one.
- Most importantly, take time to have your bath and have no fixed plans after it, because you will be very floaty and later you'll have the most restful sleep!
- Many onsen refuse entry to anyone with tattoos. If you have ink, we suggest asking your hotel or a Japanese-speaking friend to ring the establishment and ask if they allow tattoos.

西の河原公園

521-3 Kusatsu, Agatsuma-gun, Gunma

sainokawara.com/en

Naganohara-Kusatsuguchi station, then bus (30min)

SAINOKAWARA PARK
KUSATSU ONSEN

The centrepiece of Kusatsu, a small town where an array of onsen snuggle between old shops, cafes and ryokan (traditional Japanese inns), is the Yubatake, a waterway of wooden channels that inhabits the town square like a living thing. Haiku poet Basho wandered these lanes (Gunma prefecture was one of his favourite areas). He no doubt wished that he'd had a smartphone so that he could have uploaded pictures and haiku poems in praise of the Yubatake before he relaxed into his bath. The waters flow throughout the town heating schools, cafes, houses and an impressive range of onsen, each with its own unique character. Buy a special pass for access to Sainokawara Park and the two other notable onsen: Otakinoyu and Gozanoyu.

Sainokawara Park is one of our all-time favourite experiences in Japan. The walk to the spectacular rotenburo (outside bath) through rural glades, steaming pools and crumbling moss-adorned statues built up an expectation for the experience that was to follow. A simple, rustic entrance leads to enormous gender-separated pools, hewn from rock, surrounded by towering mountains and whispering pine trees. Laying back in the warm water, the vast blue sky above you, your soundtrack the melancholy calls of the circling birds, this is true relaxation in the very heart of nature.

We returned at dawn to watch the sun rise slowly over the misty mountains. The deep aquamarine of the water teamed with the dark slate of the rocks and the light hinoki-wood huts make for one of nature's most beautiful colour palettes. The benefits of Kusatsu water include healing for burns, chronic digestive diseases, chills and dermatitis, as well as being an all-round beauty treatment for your skin. As for Sainokawara Park, the benefits for the mind and spirit are immeasurable.

源氏の湯

GENJI NO YU
UJI

A short daytrip from Kyoto, Genji No Yu is a chic, architecturally designed super onsen. If you've ever wanted to immerse yourself in Murusaki Shikibu's *The Tale of Genji*, this is the place to do it as the onsen is named after the hero of Japan's famous first novel. You're likely to run into a variety of the novel's characters here on any given day. Families, couples and onsen devotees come here for the perfect daytime soak. Everything here is considered, from the chic frontage – with noren curtains and bamboo growing along the wall – to the modern lobby, friendly staff and onsen kit with super fluffy towels.

Separate male and female areas have carbolic acid water baths where tiny bubbles and herbal medicines ease your stress. The large rotenburo (outside bath) has hot-spring water piped up from over 1000 metres (3280 feet) underground, brimming with sodium and calcium chloride. It is said to be good for skin issues, aching joints and tired muscles. There are excellent cold plunge pools (locals swear by them in the steamy summer months); two saunas (one imported from Finland); and two cosy tsuberu (one-person tubs), if you feel like going solo.

Make a day of it and have lunch or dinner at the excellent Beniya (Japanese and Korean restaurant). After your bath, catch your breath in the oxygen booth or in one of the beautiful Japanese modern chillout spaces. We took a chance with the free blood-pressure tester; the results were: 'you are very relaxed'.

52 Okubo-cho, Otake,
Uji, Kyoto
genji-yu.jp
Sinden station or walk from
Okubo station (8min)

崎の湯

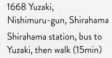

SAKI NO YU
SHIRAHAMA

Referenced in texts dating back to 658 CE, Saki No Yu is documented as Japan's oldest onsen. Set in rustic huts by the seashore, the onsen is made up of ancient sunken pools, smoothed out of the rock over time by the movement of the tide. Warm geothermal water breaks over the pools, filling them with Neptune's blessing. You'll get none of the modern comforts here, this is the real deal – uncomplicated and authentic.

Make sure to secure your valuables in a small locker outside because once inside there are open wooden boxes for your clothes and not much else. Pour warm water over yourself from fonts provided before submerging yourself in the rockpools. Baths are only metres from the roar of the ocean waves, which makes for both an exhilarating and a mesmerising experience. Gaze out to the Pacific Ocean and contemplate eternity as the waves break against the rocks, caressing your face with salty spume.

The water in Shirahama bubbles up from between two tectonic plates – you're sitting right on the fault line, adding to the primal nature of your bathing experience. The sulphur and saline water soothe neuralgia, chronic skin disease and gynaecological illnesses and make your skin softer than soft. Michelle says the girl's bath had a hinoki-wood pool which led down to several smaller baths, one attached directly to the sea. Steve saw a crab swim lazily past at one point and he thought, 'stay in the water a little longer buddy, you'll be cooked to perfection.'

1668 Yuzaki,
Nishimuru-gun, Shirahama

Shirahama station, bus to
Yuzaki, then walk (15min)

ラクーア

SPA LAQUA
TOKYO

1-1-1 Kasuga,
Bunkyo, Tokyo
laqua.jp
Korakuen station exit 2 or
Suidobashi station exit A5

It may seem incongruous to find a real onsen that pumps water up from 1700 metres (5577 feet) underground in a water-world amusement park attached to a sports and entertainment complex with a roller-coaster on the roof, but that's Tokyo. Emerging from the station to see the towering Thunder Dolphin roller-coaster weaving through a hub-less ferris wheel and practically colliding with the roof of Spa LaQua is one of those moments where the Tokyo metropolis of your imagination comes screaming to life (literally).

LaQua is an adult-only affair: there is no entry to children under five years old, and older children are only allowed access with grown-ups. Baths are gender-segregated and include jet baths, a 42°C (107°F) cypress bath and a rockpool (running at a much more comfortable 38°C/100°F). Outside, there are two fine rotenburo baths and a footbath complete with TV. All water is sodium chloride, great for smooth skin, relaxation and easing stiff muscles.

If you're a sauna connoisseur, there are three steam rooms in the main area but we recommend paying extra yen for the Healing Baden. There are many different saunas themed to different countries and eras which have different beneficial effects, such as anti-ageing and increased blood circulation.

The vast relaxation space allows you to lie back on couches or comfortable reclining seats while reading magazines, watching TV or listening to music. Order food, drinks and delicious desserts, unwind or take a nap. Inside, you'll feel the city's madness float away.

MINDFUL TIP
After a soak, visit beautiful nearby Koishikawa Korakuen garden (see p.163).

銀山温泉

GINZAN ONSEN
OBANAZAWA

Ginzan Onsen (Silver Mountain Hot Spring) in Obanazawa is named after the nearby silver mine that dates back some 500 years. It's a rare Taisho-period town (1912 to 1926, an equivalent of the Art Deco era) sunken into a valley and flowing with some of Japan's most beneficial waters.

A stayover in Ginzan is truly unique – especially in winter when it's rugged and frozen, difficult but spectacular. Strolling along Ginzan's main street, lined on both sides with highly ornate historic inns overlooking picturesque bridges spanning the Ginzan River, will make you feel like you've travelled through time. When icicles hang from the eaves and snow is heavy on the rooftops and thick alongside the river, Ginzan is a fairytale wonderland. Walking through the narrow streets late at night, when the bridges and walkways are illuminated by gas lamps and ryokan (traditional Japanese inn) guests are strolling in their yukata (summer cotton kimono), is a magical experience.

Ginzan's onsen are mostly inside ryokan, however many are available for day bathers. If you're visiting for the day you will have access to three inexpensive public baths: Kengo Kuma's minimal, contemporary bath Shiroganeyu; Kajikayu; and Omokageyu. Soak your tired feet in Ginzan's warashiyu (footbath) while taking in the town's precious scenery and admiring the kote-e art that master plasterers have applied to panels on buildings.

Ginzan Onsen Tourist Information

429 Ginzanshinhata, Obanazawa, Yamagata-ken

Oishida station, then bus (35min)

MINDFUL TIP

For lovers of Kuma, don't miss the striking Ginzan Onsen Fujiya Inn, a modern and highly architectural addition to the Taisho-period streetscape.

蔵王温泉大露天風呂

853 Zao Onsen,
Yamagata

Yamagata station, then
bus to Zao Onsen

ZAO DAI-ROTENBURO

ZAO ONSEN

Cradled between Yamagata and Miyagi, Zao Onsen is one of Japan's top ski resorts. It also features many geological wonders. Mount Zao's Okama crater ('Japan's cooking pot') is a picturesque crater lake inside an active volcano. In winter, Zao's trees are famous for becoming pudgy with snow and taking on the appearance of a host of ethereal snow spectres. The abundance of nature, greenery and the changing hues of the foliage make Zao perfect for lovers of the great outdoors. It also holds one of Japan's unmissable onsen.

Closed in winter due to the dangerous snows, Zao Dai-Rotenburo is a picture-perfect outdoor bath with a secret history spanning a rumoured 1900 years. The onsen's pools of shimmering blue water are set in a lush ravine amongst the wooded glades of the linden trees. We wore the yukata (summer cotton kimono) from our ryokan (traditional Japanese inn) and walked up the steep slope in our geta (wooden clogs), towels in hand, click-clacking on the path, careful not to slip on the roadway that was slick with errant mineral-rich thermal water which flowed from pipes and drains. We made our way down through the canopied entrance, balancing precariously on the steep steps until we arrived at the front of the forested onsen. The spacious rockpools collected rich warm water as it cascaded into the valley. The lazy buzz of summer insects and the chirp of birds soundtracked our bath and mingled with the perfumes of the forest and light scent of the water. The water boasts the highest acidity level in Japan with a pH nearing 1 – a concentration that imbues your skin with softness and an intensely vibrant glow. The water here is also known for relieving chronic skin conditions, hypertension, diabetes and muscle pain.

Baths are gender separated and tattoos are allowed. Zao Onsen town also features three smaller local bathhouses. Take advantage of the three-onsen pass for a discounted fee and avail yourself of the premium water.

乳頭温泉郷 鶴の湯温泉

50, Sendatsu, Tazawako,
Tazawa, Senbokushi, Akita
tsurunoyu.com/english.html
Tazawako station Ugo Kotsu
bus to Arupa Komakusa

TSURU NO YU

NYUTO ONSEN

A samurai roadside pitstop, Tsuru No Yu is cradled by the glorious mountains of the Towada-Hachimantai National Park. The oldest of the onsen in Nyuto (picture a time when merchants would haul their goods along dusty trails until they were desperately in need of a bath), Tsuru No Yu's charred wood buildings of astounding rustic beauty seem to emerge organically from the lush vegetation.

Day bathing is available, so make new friends and join in the jovial, ebullient chatter while you soak your cares away. However, we adamantly recommend staying overnight in the Edo-period (1603 to 1867) wooden lodgings. We chose a room with a traditional irori fireplace, where dinner was cooked for us over the flame using locally sourced ingredients. Our day was spent bathing, relaxing and exploring the grounds clad in yukata (summer cotton kimono). At night, as the lamps turned on, the mountain air was full of perfumed flowers and the sweet smell of sulphur. We awoke at 3am, intent on a moonlight bath and a walk along the deserted lamp-lit pathways.

Small gender-separated and private baths can be found amongst the labyrinthine corridors of the ryokan (traditional Japanese inn), but the main onsen is the star of the show. It's the stuff of folklore – trees reveal glimpses of a smooth milky white pool of steaming hot, sulphurous water, bordered by wooden huts, towering reeds and rocky outcrops. The bath is mixed, with separate entrance points for men and women. Women can ease themselves into the opaque water from the privacy of a large rock, surrounded in the summer months by blooming hydrangeas. Once in the water, all cares slip away as the healing water does its work and nano bubbles emerge from underground and tickle your skin. The sun sinking behind the misty mountains or rising in a blood-red morning sky are atmospheric scenes that will forever be the backdrop of your onsen bathing memories.

法師温泉長寿館

650 Nagai, Minakami,
Tone-gun

hoshi-onsen.com/english

Jomokogen station then
bus to Sarugakyo, then
Hoshi shuttle

HOSHI ONSEN CHOJUKAN

HOSHI ONSEN, MINAKAMI

Hoshi Onsen is one of ten 'secret' onsens of Japan, hidden in the green depths
of the Joshin'etsukogen National Park. Hoshi's rokumeikan-style (Meiji-period
westernised-style) building has a stunning dark wooden exterior accented by
flecks of green foliage in summer or transformed into a wonderland in the winter
snows. If you want to discover a deeper omotenashi (Japanese hospitality), you've
come to the right place.

Once inside, you'll feel like you've been taken back to simpler, better times.
The architecture echoes the bygone railways of 19th-century Japan. Winding
corridors with low ceilings feature faded photographs and glass cases with a blend
of oddments, fossil shells retrieved from the soil, 1960s shinkansen (bullet train)
models and beautiful antique fans and fabrics – all which help unravel Hoshi's
fascinating history.

'Hoshi no yu' is 140 years old, a Meiji-period (1868 to 1912) onsen featuring a
grid of baths bordered by wood, languishing under a breathtaking vaulted wooden
ceiling. Light diffused through arched and square slatted windows gives the
room the appearance of a chapel and, why not, this onsen feels like a religious
experience. It's a mixed bath, the separate men's and women's changing rooms
lead into the central room (the bath is for women only between 8pm and 10pm).
The water here is rare – it bubbles up from the gaps in the stones, caressing you
with rich minerals. The calcium, sodium sulphate and gypsum help aid the healing
of injuries, burns, gastrointestinal issues and arteriosclerosis.

A limited day-bathing schedule is available with lunch included, however staying
overnight here is a once-in-a-lifetime experience. It's breathtaking from the
moment you set foot inside the low-lit reception to the moment you bow your
goodbyes. Never have we been so looked after, slept so soundly and felt so relaxed.

山河旅館

RYOKAN SANGA
KUROKAWA ONSEN

6961-1 Minamioguni, Manganji
Aso-Gun, Kumamoto
sanga-ryokan.com/en
Kurokawa Onsen bus stop,
then shuttle

Kurokawa Onsen in the heart of Kyushu is a 300-year-old onsen town lost in the mountains, barely touched by modern life and channelling the true spirit of the Edo period (1603 to 1867). There are 21 inns that line the Chikugo River, each with a memorable onsen experience to be cherished during an overnight stay or as a day visitor.

Ryokan Sanga is an enchanting inn with a large garden where nooks and crannies hide onsen in fairytale-like huts, ponds ripple with gently drifting koi and smoke rises from wood-fired kitchens with cast-iron kettles hung low over burning cedar. At night lantern-lit pathways guide you around small houses, enchanting in winter's soft falling snow or the cool of the summer night air. Sanga's main building has 20th-century charm, many winding corridors with polished wood floors, secret alcoves and a small library and relaxation room complete with fireplace and coffee bar.

The main onsen, Moyainoyu, is a mixed bath in a small grotto with steaming water cascading from pipes, rocks peeking out from the surface of the water and rustic bath bowls. The water is famed for its powers of rejuvenation. Women have their own cosy outdoor bath, called Shikinoyu. There are two gender-segregated indoor baths and three private baths, all containing sweetly sulphurous water. If you get the chance to spend the night here, it's an experience you will never forget.

竹瓦温泉

TAKEGAWARA ONSEN
BEPPU

16-23 Motomachi,
Beppu, Oita

Beppu station, then
walk (15min)

In a town where there are plenty of bathing experiences, small and large baths and modern baths in ryokan (traditional Japanese inns) or hotels, Takegawara stands out – an impressive local favourite, secreted in Beppu's network of backstreets and lanes. You'll be immediately drawn to the arresting ornate frontage, the beautiful curve of the entrance canopy, the Chinese-style gabled roof and the warm light diffusing through the latticed windows. The large, picturesque entrance is a mix of old and new, a marker of the early Showa period (1926 to 1989) when the bathhouse was built (1938).

The inviting lobby features beautiful dark rich woods and high ceilings, wooden floors buffed to a gleam, low yellow lights and an evocative lattice roof. Inside, the onsen is rustic with wooden lockers and shabby chic stained and cracked tiles painted with mineral salts – you can almost count the layers to reveal the age of the bathhouse. It's intimate and small. The water is hot, drawn up from Beppu's bounteous geothermal vents. Ghosts of steam rise up and waft around you. If you're lucky, the self-proclaimed master and mistress of the bathhouse will give you unsolicited advice on your bathing skills.

Upstairs you'll find a unique Kyushu experience. Assistants dig a hole and then bury you up to your neck in dark rich sand warmed by pipes filled with onsen water (you are horizontal and wearing a robe). Just lie back and enjoy the warmth as toxins leach from your body.

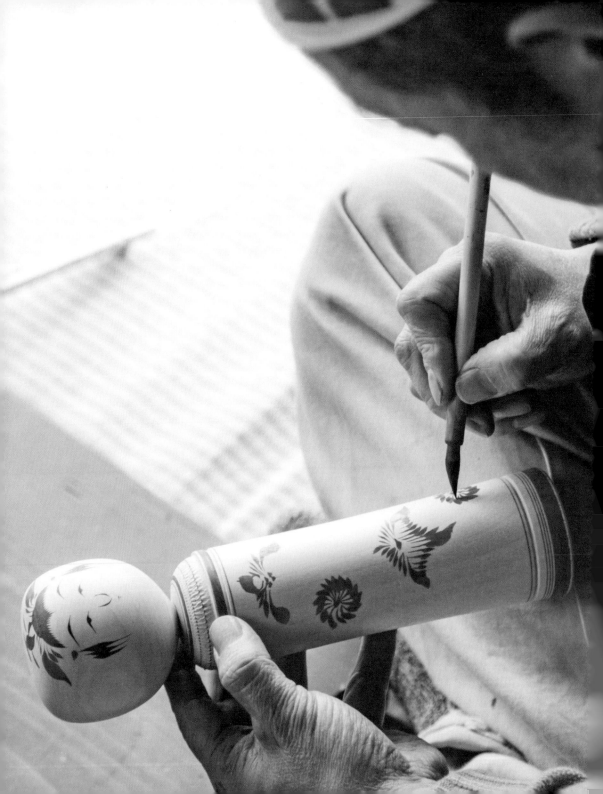

心を満たすクリエイティブな体験

Mindful
creative
experiences

We've long held a deep admiration for Japanese artisan crafts. As avid buyers of vintage and small-maker items we are in awe of the dedication and skill of local craftspeople. One of our reasons for returning to Japan time and time again is the joy of visiting new prefectures and small towns and seeking out their local specialties.

The Japanese have a word, 'kodowari', that expresses a deep devotion and single-minded application to one's calling. This is adopted wholeheartedly by the Japanese artisan. Throughout the history of the Japanese periods, master craftspeople honed their skills taking ideas from China and beyond, reinventing and perfecting them for a Japanese audience of emperors and samurai. Families known for a particular craft passed their intricate skills and secrets down through the generations. Crafted objects were highly valued and looked upon as the supreme expression of an artisan's skill.

Michelle has a particular obsession with the three beautiful arts taught to refined women in ancient Japan. The art of kodo (incense) is known as the way of fragrance, a technique where you 'listen' to perfectly composed scents. Chado is the art of the tea ceremony (see p. 39) and ikebana (kado) is the way of the flowers (see p. 84), and are both processes that require intense concentration, deep study and a humble spirit.

Craft in Japan includes ironware, ceramics and pottery, textile design and print, shibori (textile dyeing), boro (upcycled textiles), lacquerware, papermaking, kintsugi (the art of visible repair) and wood carving. Walking into a craft-person's studio, watching the concentration of the potter, or admiring the deft swish of the calligrapher's brush instantly puts you in touch with a simpler time and inspires personal satisfaction through creativity.

Shodo (calligraphy) was introduced to Japan from China in the Asuka period (538 to 710 CE). Buddhist temples in Mount Koya and Kyoto have a long history of calligraphy. Ikebana began in the Heian period (794 to 1185 CE). Ikebana has very distinctive schools of thought both in Tokyo and Kyoto. The art of kintsugi originated in the Muromachi period (1336 to 1573 CE); shibori, which also originated from China, became popular in the Edo period (1603 to 1867 CE), rising to fame in Arimatsu, a town on the road from Kyoto to Tokyo.

In our modern era of mass production, artisan crafts remain highly regarded. Younger generations in Japan find that the allure of single-mindedness, skill and simplicity resonates in the face of a more automated world. Sustainability and a move away from single-use items is high on the agenda. New artisans have a deep reverence for centuries of tradition and source their materials locally, imbuing their objects with harmony and balance and a lyrical quality that only a truly organic process can create.

Previous: Sakurai Kokeshi; *opposite top left:* Japanese paint store; *opposite top right and bottom* Kintsugi lessons at Kuge Crafts

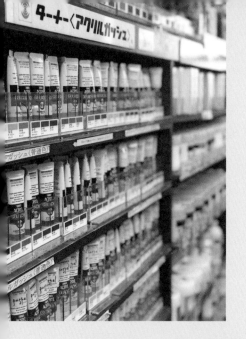

山田松香木店

164 Kageyukojicho,
Kamigyo-ku, Kyoto

Marutamachi station exit 2,
then walk (5min)

INCENSE CLASSES AT YAMADA-MATSU
KYOTO

Our first trip to Kyoto was a feast for the senses. Impeccable food, Buddhist temple bells and elegant gardens. Our strongest memory, however, was the incense. It wafts through the Kyoto streets, evoking deep emotions, a heady mix of wood, florals and smoke. A perfectly balanced scent makes your heart take flight, transports you to another time or place and fills you with an inner peace.

Incense arrived from China in the Asuka period (538 to 710 CE); and in the Heian period (794 to 1185 CE) it wafted out of the temples and into Court. The Muromachi period (1336 to 1573 CE) created kodo (the way of fragrance). In the Edo period (1603 to 1867 CE), samurai used incense as a mindful practice before battle.

Dating back 200 years, Yamada-Matsu started out as a pharmacy that sold quality wood and raw ingredients for making incense. These essentials are now displayed in small drawers and jars in their exquisite store. A stunning wood exterior with mustard noren curtains leads you inside where incense crafting tools and materials are displayed like museum pieces. Stylishly packaged incense sticks and sachets with unique and alluring scents are ready to take home so holiday memories can waft back into your daily life.

Yamada-Matsu hold three styles of Monko (the art of enjoying incense) workshops. Assemble a censer (small ceramic vessel), ending with cupped hands over the vessel, learning how to 'listen' to the fragrance. Make scented sachets, perfect for drawers and to use as a natural insect repellent or learn how to make kneaded incense by fashioning powder with special syrup. Kneaded balls are then heated with charcoal to enjoy the fragrance in a room. Workshops run for 50 minutes to an hour. Book online (yamadamatsu.co.jp/en). Kindly refrain from wearing fragrance to class.

京都絞り工芸館

127 Shikiamicho,
Nakagyo-ku, Kyoto
Karasuma-Oike station,
then walk (10min)

KYOTO SHIBORI MUSEUM

KYOTO

We've always collected vintage shibori textiles for their beauty: colour and fleeting interplay between fabric and ink. The art of shibori was popularised in the Edo period (1603 to 1867 CE). Classic indigo or coloured dyes produce exquisite patterns on silk hemp and cotton using knotting, pleating, pinching and stitching techniques that bind the cloth, giving it a resistance to dye.

The Kyoto Shibori Museum is a startlingly contemporary building. Blue in colour, geometric in design, this is contemporary architecture in perfect harmony with its habitat – a museum in an ancient capital, dedicated to the 1300-year-old art form of tie-dyeing textiles.

You can choose from four classes at the museum, each resulting in a piece you can wear, cherish or give as that perfect gift. Make your own shibori long silk scarf in one of the three half-hour classes, each specialising in a different dyeing method: Itajime-shibori (multiple coloured patterned technique), Kyo-arashi-shibori (folding technique with one colour) or Sekka-shibori (snow crystal one-colour technique). The intermediate 60 to 90 minute Fukusa-shibori masterclass specialises in winding and knotting, teaching you how to make the city's famous dappled pattern on a piece of square silk fabric.

While your creation dries, wander the museum's permanent exhibit of Kyoto-style dyeing (Kyo-kanoko-shibori). Exit the gift store on the way out filled with shibori products and accessories. In a world of throwaway fast fashion, making your own furoshiki or tenagui wrap (sustainable cloth wrapping for presents) makes for a mindful eco holiday. Lessons can be booked online (en.shibori.jp).

退蔵院

CALLIGRAPHY AT TAIZOIN TEMPLE
KYOTO

35, Hanazono, Myoshinji-cho, Ukyo-ku, Kyoto

JR Sagano line to Hanazono station, then walk (10min)

Imagine that you can conjure up depth of feeling and expression within a masterful brush stroke, expressing thoughts and ideas through a simple, beautifully realised set of Kanji. Japanese shodo (calligraphy) was greatly influenced by the work of Chinese master Wang Xizhi in the 4th century but moved into its own sphere when Japanese script was developed. Zen philosophy added a whole new dimension to calligraphy, imbuing it with a spiritual, poetic potency.

On the grounds of Kyoto's Taizoin, a kind of calm washes over you. The stunning Zen temple dates to 1404 CE, a sub-temple of the vast Myoshinji Temple complex. In addition to the impressive temple buildings, it has two perfectly opposing dry gardens: 'Inyou no Niwa', a dark rock dry garden and a light rock dry garden, reflecting duality. We always think of them as the yin of the 21st century contrasting with the yang of the temple's history.

Wander through the grounds, making time for a bowl of matcha and wagashi (Japanese sweets) in the teahouse 'Daikyuan', before joining the calligraphy class, beautifully situated on the temple grounds. A Zen monk describes the history of calligraphy before teaching you how to master the fearless strokes of 'bokuseki' (Zen-infused calligraphy) that transports Kanji to a divine plane. The lesson takes an hour and a half and includes a tour of historical calligraphy works on display at the temple. Taizoin also has zazen (meditation) classes and a Japanese tea experience. Book online (taizoin.com) and make sure to enquire about accommodation at the temple.

頂法寺 六角堂

248 Donomae-cho,
Rokkaku-dori, Higashinotoin,
Nishi-iru, Nakagyo-ku, Kyoto
Karasuma Oike station, then
walk (5min)

IKENOBO AT ROKKAKUDO CHOHOJI TEMPLE
KYOTO

One of the highest forms of mindful practice in Japan, ikebana combines the spiritual teachings of Buddhism with the careful placement of bud, branch and stem. Over 550 years ago, Senno Ikenobo developed a philosophy that formed the basis of ikebana. In stark contrast to Western flower arranging, it's a meditation on form, evoking the flower's inner beauty and spirit to present the fragility of nature in a precious tableau.

Rokkakudo, the birthplace of ikebana, is an atmospheric temple in the backstreets of Kyoto dating back 1400 years. The temple is lush with weeping trees and clipped pine, and in sakura (cherry blossom) season, the pink bloom of perfectly placed cherry trees becomes a living ikebana display.

Learning the gentle way of the flower from the masters at Ikenobo was the highlight of our first trip to Kyoto. Instructors teach a two-hour free-form class allowing budding artisans to arrange their own branches and blooms. At the end of the lesson your 'sensei' will glide around the room, making a slight adjustment to a branch or tweaking a leaf until, suddenly, your arrangement comes to life. The lesson finishes with tea and wagashi (Japanese sweets). Classes are intimate and conducted on Thursdays between 1.30 and 3.30pm. A modest dress code is encouraged.

Enquire about the temple tour (in English) when you book your class online (ikenobo.jp/english). At the store you can buy a set of ikebana tools to continue your mastery at home. We always burn Rokkakudo's unique incense at home and are instantly transported back to these magical grounds.

越前和紙の里

8-44 Shinzaike-cho,
Echizen, Fukui

echizenwashi.jp

Takefu station, then bus to
Washi-no-Sato (20min)

ECHIZEN WASHI (PAPER) VILLAGE
FUKUI

Paper folding artform devotees, avid diary writers, obsessive snail mailers and watercolour enthusiasts take note – paper paradise awaits. Picture perfect, surrounded by mountains and forests, inhabited by glorious trees and waterways and historic architecture, Washi-no-Sato (Echizen Washi Village) is a pilgrimage every analogue correspondence obsessive needs to go on. Consider spending the night so you can wander the town at your own leisurely pace.

Your first stop should be Udatsu Paper and Craft Museum, a papermaker's house that dates back to 1748 with an extensive display of the washi paper made in the village's 67 paper mills. Book online two weeks in advance (echizenwashi.jp) for one of the papermaking courses using traditional techniques. Learn about hosho (wrapping paper), gasenshi (calligraphy paper), kyokushi (watercolour paper and postcards) and other specialty paper forms.

Don't miss a visit to the studio of the Iwano family, designated as a Living National Treasure for being ninth-generation papermakers. Their specialty mulberry bark (kozo) paper is made with a centuries-old techniques and it is inspiring to watch the family's skills in action.

MINDFUL TIP

Take the country path to a forest bathed in dappled light, alive with the sounds of nature, to worship the paper goddess Kawakami Gozen at the rustic Okamoto Otaki shrine.

We spent a joyous day here wandering the streets, popping into craft studios and watching the masters work. Michelle tried to not overspend her paper budget while daydreaming about her next paper project. Bring your own cloth bag to house your purchases. Buying artisan pieces supports local business and fits with a sustainable and mindful holiday.

たくみの里

847 Sukawa, Minakami,
Tone-gun, Gunma

Jomokogen station, then
Numata-Sarugakyo bus
(20min)

TAKUMINOSATO CRAFT VILLAGE
TAKUMINOSATO, MINAKAMI

Reset your mind to village life. The echo of a hammer's fall, the clack of the loom, the lazy drone of insects in summer and the delighted squeals of children as they target each other with freshly packed snowballs in winter. Takuminosato is just such a time and place. The village is home to a variety of hand-crafters and makers and is a haven for anyone who still lives by the ideal that, if it isn't made with your hands it isn't made with love. There are artisan workshops dotted amongst apple orchards and rice fields, all hugged by Minakami's sleepy mountains.

Recognising Michelle's deep love of craft, our friend Yuko introduced us to Takuminosato. We strolled from workshop to workshop partaking in classes, most of which take around an hour. The extensive art and craft on offer includes zōri (woven straw sandal) making, bamboo weaving, indigo dyeing and candle and washi papermaking. You can even fold, roll and cut your own soba noodles (and of course eat them). We watched a local artisan potter working the wheel and silk being woven on the loom. Steve tried his hand at making his own personalised stamp, while Michelle painted a fan and bought three pairs of the rustic zori for herself and as presents for loved ones.

Later, we slipped into Shiki no Ie (House of the Four Seasons), an Edo-period (1603 to 1867) eatery specialising in soba with edible wild plants, and watched the fireflies dance in the dark outside – the perfect end to a day experiencing old village life.

古民家古木

3288-6 Mashiko,
Mashiko-machi,
Haga-gun, Tochigi

Kanto Yakimono Liner
(Pottery Bus) from Akihabara
station (3hr) or Kanto bus
from Utsunomiya for Mashiko
(50min), then walk (5min)
from Sankokan Mae stop

POTTERY AT MINSHUKU FURUKI

MASHIKO

Rustic accommodation with ceramic kilns and classes, Minshuku Furuki is a country haven for the promising potter. A three-hour bus trip from Tokyo on the 'Pottery Line', Mashiko is one of Japan's most revered pottery towns. Their traditional pottery style, Mashiko-yaki, is made from the town's abundant silicic acid and iron-rich soil, which produces ceramics in the palest of neutrals, clay and chalk and the deep darks of mud and charcoal. Glazing colours include stone whites through to persimmon, deep blues and blacks. Mashiko's distinctive style dates back to the 8th century CE, however it wasn't until 1930 when Shoji Hamada, a leading light in the mingei (folk craft movement), made Mashiko famous with his contemporary style.

Mayu and Issei Furuki run a a minshuku (bed and breakfast) in a 300-year-old farmhouse with its own kiln where you can feel your creative senses awaken with the sounds of birds. We love the rustic rooms, communal cooking and lounge areas where you can gather and talk about the shape and texture of your creation. Their small English-friendly classes go for 90 minutes, 3 hours (morning or afternoon) or a full day and are held in a rustic barn, with pottery wheels lined up for novice creatives to shape their clay before choosing a glaze.

Explore the town with their free hire bikes to visit pottery studios, large noborigama (climbing) kilns and the Shoji Hamada Museum. Watch potters sculpt their forms and bake them in one of the town's 300 working kilns. If you can't wait for your pottery to be fired, your hosts will mail home your creation!

桜井こけし店

Yumoto 26, Naruko Onsen,
Osaki, Miyagi

en.sakuraikokeshiten.com

Naruko Onsen station,
then walk (3min)

SAKURAI KOKESHI WORKSHOP
NARUKO ONSEN

Michelle has been collecting kokeshi dolls from vintage markets in Japan for
years, looking for the perfect handpainted face and artfully patterned body.
Her friend Makiko, who lives in the Tohoku region, suggested a trip to Naruko in
Miyagi prefecture which is, according to local legend, the birthplace of kokeshi
in the Edo period (1603 to 1867). The town features kokeshi-themed postboxes,
telephone booths, manhole covers and a kokeshi museum.

Kokeshi are an abstracted human form with a round head on a cylindrical body.
The process of harvesting the wood, drying, turning and then deftly painting the
face and body is a skill years in the making. In a world of mass-produced toys
these one-of-a kind dolls made by locals are the perfect mindful present.

The Sakurai family have made kokeshi since the late 1800s. They are the oldest
of the 20 maker families in Naruko. Their multi-award-winning fifth-generation
craft-person, Akihiro Sakurai carries on the family tradition as well as crafting
his own unique dolls. Their beautiful Edo-period store is crammed with shelves
and tables of dolls in all shapes, colours and sizes. We particularly loved the fluoro
dolls, unlike anything we had seen before.

Sakurai share their intimate knowledge by offering kokeshi painting classes.
Bookable on their English-friendly website or as a walk-up on the day (weekends
are busy), it takes between half an hour to an hour to complete your masterpiece,
imbuing your Tohoku-shaped doll (we recommend this style), kokeshi pen stand
or greeting kokeshi with its own personality, colour story and mood.

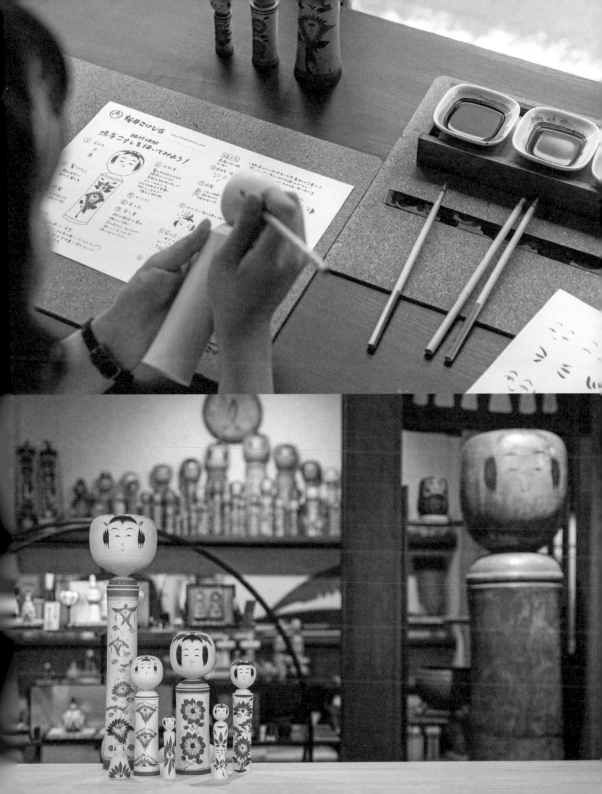

手仕事屋久家

1-34-10 Narita-higashi,
Suginami-ku, Tokyo
Shin-Koenji station exit 1,
then walk (8min)

KINTSUGI AT KUGE CRAFTS
TOKYO

Tucked away in the backstreets of Tokyo's Koenji neighbourhood is a craft studio dedicated to broken things and the beauty of showing flaws. In an area famous for its vintage fashion, relaxed local vibes and eclectic residents, Kuge Crafts teaches the golden art of visible repair on pottery and porcelain. In stark contrast to many Western values, the art of kintsugi celebrates the life of an object and to repair rather than discard. It's one of Japan's finest examples of the principle of wabi-sabi, the acceptance of imperfection, and of mottainai, expressing the regret in wastage – the equivalent of sustainable mending.

We attended a workshop with our dear friend Hiki who surprised us with the gift of learning an express version of kintsugi from Yoshiichiro sensei and Yoshiko sensei, who have taught ceramics for over 35 years. On arrival we were greeted with tea and sweets, before choosing from a range of cups and bowls with small chips. Hiki brought a treasured plate which had been broken, we chose a piece each based on intuition and began the process of giving our objects a new life. We set about moulding epoxy (non-toxic) into the break. When it hardened, we filed it, then painted it with lacquer before sprinkling on metallic gold powder.

The visible mending of a broken object gives it a melancholy beauty – a compelling metaphor for how highlighting the damage defiantly shows the history of the break, imbuing it with new meaning.

Kuge classes go for 2.5 hours and are English friendly. Book online (teshigotoya-kuge.com) in advance.

信州土産店たかぎ

TEMARI BALL WORKSHOP AT TAKAGI
MATSUMOTO

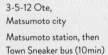

The castle town of Matsumoto has a deep affinity with craft. It hosts the biggest craft fair in Japan, Crafts Fair Matsumoto, which takes place around the end of May each year. The shops along the historic streets are dedicated to various crafts, including lacquer, bamboo craft, wood-carving, sake and miso making and the colourful Temari ball.

Legend has it that over 200 years ago, the first Temari ball was created by the wife of a Matsumoto noble. Originally intended to be a toy for children, the Temari, tightly wound from silk yarn, has since become a talisman of peace and harmony, often gifted by a bride to her groom's family.

3-5-12 Ote,
Matsumoto city
Matsumoto station, then
Town Sneaker bus (10min)

Takagi have Temari ball workshops that let you become part of this story. An old curiosity shop of souvenirs and keepsakes, they have been making and selling Temari since 1878 in the late Edo period (1603 to 1867). Their three-hour workshops guide you through the intricate process of choosing the thread, working out the geometry and colours and plotting your design. Book your three-hour workshop one week in advance (ask a Japanese speaker to call 0263 32 5337).

You can also order a cheeky drink at Beer Happy on the roof terrace (April to Sept), although make sure you do this after the class to avoid wonky patterns on your Temari! Be sure to leave time to explore the town's backstreets.

MINDFUL TIP
Temari balls are so entrenched in the town's history that they are featured in its manhole cover designs.

心を満たす食事

Mindful
eating

One of the things we travel to Japan for is undoubtedly the food. Elevated yet humble, healthy and considered, Japanese food is complex in its simplicity. The term mindfulness couldn't be more apt for the country's cuisine. Everything you eat puts you in the moment. The beauty in food presentation is matched by its healthy and diverse ingredients. Each delicate dish or brimming bowl is designed with flavour, nutrition and presentation in mind.

Travelling for food has taken us well beyond the clichés. Try everything – local, seasonal specialties; shojin ryori temple feasts or kaiseki ryori banquets; creative uses of staples like rice, noodles and broths; craft beer and sake – and you will quickly find that the range and quality is truly impressive. As a designer, Michelle adores wagashi, delicate sweets, seasonally flavoured and sculpted into formations that resemble flora, fauna and abstract works of art. Steve loves eating at food markets and waking to a traditional Japanese breakfast.

Japanese cuisine can be one of the healthiest in the world. There is a phrase, 'Hara Hachi Bu', meaning to eat until you are 80 per cent full, an interesting philosophy that ensures that the body only takes in what it needs. The bento box and small-plate concept mean that food is naturally portion controlled. A fish- and rice-based food culture allows for nutritious and vitamin-rich eating.

The Japanese know how to imbue even the humblest food with a sense of occasion. You can be in a high-end sushi restaurant sampling delicate morsels a la carte or in a ryokan (traditional Japanese inn) enjoying a kaiseki banquet, on a train eating a bento box or eating a tasty ramen in a standing bar surrounded by slurping salarymen – no matter what or where the experience, you'll be imprinting a lasting food memory.

THE FIVE COLOURS OF JAPANESE CUISINE

Nature's colours make their way into the core philosophy behind Japanese food. To eat from nature's palette means you will eat a well-balanced meal for health and wellbeing. Rustic earthenware and lacquerware brings out the beauty of the food's colours and textures. Seasonally coloured foods add joy to festivals and special occasions. During sakura (cherry blossom) season, for example, most things will come in pink – from sweets to beer!

Previous: Vegetable display in Kyoto; *opposite top left:* Wrapped freshly made bento boxes; *opposite top right:* Taiyaki street stall; *opposite bottom:* Aomori apples

地鶏めし　870円

大極殿六角店 栖園

120 Horinoe-cho, Rokkaku dori
Nakagyo-ku, Kyoto
Kurasum-Oike station exit 5,
then walk (5min)

SEIEN AT DAIGOKUDEN HONPO
KYOTO

Opening in 1885, Daigokuden Kyoto store is where the locals go to buy sweets for special occasions. When strolling down Rokkaku dori we have always admired the building. Its vintage exterior of traditional Kyoto architecture features koshi (wooden slat windows) suffusing warm light, an ornate mushiko (insect cage) wooden window that spans the entire frontage and noren curtains that change colour and design with the seasons.

Inside, antique cabinets are filled with tiny delights, including an extensive range of the specialty higashi (sweet cakes) pressed and shaped in kashigata (traditional sweets moulds) and made into brightly coloured seasonal and symbolic shapes used for events, tea ceremonies and shrine offerings. Beautifully packaged, they make the perfect gifts to take home to friends.

Internal tearoom Seien is famous for its Kohaku Nagashi, agar jelly with seasonal fruit syrup which changes flavours on a monthly basis (reflected in the changing noren curtains). We've tried amazake syrup in March, plum liquor in June, chestnut in October and persimmon in November. Sencha and matcha are also served with zenzai, small islands of mochi (sweet rice cakes) floating in warm red-bean soup. You can meditate upon the artful creation of your sweets while gazing at the tearoom's delicate garden featuring goldfish in water bowls, small rockeries and sprays of vibrant green moss.

On a trip with friends, Michelle hoped to visit for tea and sweets, however the store was closed that day. The owner was sweeping outside and noticed their disappointment. She promptly went inside and gifted them some sweets to try.

ひろ文

8-7 Kuramakibune-cho
Sakyo-ku, Kyoto

Kibune-Guchi station,
then walk or taxi (5min)

HIROBUN KAWADOKO DINING
KIBUNE

A picturesque town in northern Kyoto, Kibune's central road winds through thickly
forested mountains that smell of fresh cedar and trill with birdsong. Shops selling
trinkets and souvenirs line the strip and daytrippers lick soft-serve ice-cream
while watching the hypnotic moss-covered waterwheel outside Kibune onsen
complete its revolutions.

In the early throws of summer when the heat starts to set in, restaurants along
the river set up platforms across the water for a memorable outdoor dining
experience called kawadoko. Hirobun's delectable kaiseki set banquets are
served in the fresh mountain air. We sat cross-legged on zabuton (floor cushions),
surrounded by red umbrellas and under a lantern-strewn bamboo canopy. On
the platform suspended over the water we caught the spray from waterfalls and
listened to the river rushing beneath us.

Two-tiered lacquer bento boxes held many small-dish delicacies including
blistered and skewered ayu (sweetfish). We ate a range of delectable mountain
vegetable dishes, sashimi, rice and pickles. Lunch included the fun nagashi somen
course, where soba noodles slide in water down bamboo pipes and you gather
them up with your chopsticks before eating them.

Kawadoko dining usually takes place from May to September, but it is dependent
on the moods of the weather. There are a variety of eateries specialising in
different types of food and each has a different riverscape and their own style
of colourful lanterns which, when lit up at night, make for a very romantic dining
experience. Book ahead online for dinner (hirobun.co.jp), but at lunchtime
take your chances (arrive early or you will have to queue). Also note: only
cash is accepted.

陶泉 御所坊

TOCEN GOSHOBO
ARIMA ONSEN

858 Arima-cho,
Kita-ku, Kobe

Arima Onsen station,
then walk (5min)

Arima Onsen town dates back over 1000 years and proudly lays claim to being one of the oldest onsen destinations in Japan. A hilly, strollable hamlet less than an hour from Kyoto, Arima features spring sources, steaming wellsprings, pipes and drains bubbling and smouldering with the region's golden, iron-rich water.

Tocen Goshobo (established 1191 CE), now in its 16th generation of ownership, has long been a place of deep spiritual contemplation, visited by samurai, writers, poets and artisans. It's an upscale ryokan (traditional Japanese inn) offering accommodation and a set lunch and bathing options. We noticed their intricate logo design while researching their food and realised they approached everything with the same attention to detail. We booked for Boxing Day lunch as a Christmas present to ourselves and ordered our food online in advance. It's a clever life hack to book a set lunch in a renowned place that may otherwise be out of your budget for dinner or an overnight stay.

With its roots in the Kamakura period (1192 to 1333 CE), Tocen Goshobo was present at the very inception of kaiseki-style cuisine and showcases an array of tempting small dishes that befits the inn's status as a vacation destination for lords and emperors. Impossibly immaculate staff in kimono float into exquisite rooms and present you with delicacies in jewel boxes and refined tableware. Relax in the salon/library or prop yourself up at the bar which serves the region's best sake. For lunch, Michelle chose the hand-cut soba noodles with tempura, Steve the Kobe beef stew. Both dishes came with an array of sides showcasing the blessings of the mountain and the abundance of the sea.

MINDFUL TIP

Literature fans note. Goshobo was a favourite haunt of *In Praise of Shadows* author Junichiro Tanizaki.

After lunch don't miss Goshobo's onsen, sex-segregated rockpools brimming with Arima's famous water. A twist has the dividing wall between the two pools get lower as you near the far end. Eventually you'll find yourself in a mixed-gender bath. Choose your own mood, privacy or lively over-the-wall conversation. Day plans are also available including lunch and a hot springs bath. Book online (goshoboh.com) in advance.

スターダスト

STARDUST
KYOTO

41 Shichi-ku,
Shimotakedono-cho,
Kita-ku, Kyoto
Kitaoiji station,
then walk (30min)

Wander Kyoto's beautiful north, where the locals go about their days and the narrow streets are filled with small maker and mom and pop stores. You'll discover a slow-living Kyoto, leaving the busy city centre and crowded temples far behind.

At Stardust, time moves differently. It's a hybrid of a delicate and precious cafe and a store selling beautiful things, where nature embellishes the darkly atmospheric space, balls of moss form on concrete and tendrils of greenery weave in and out of the room. Flora and fauna displays, brass, crystals and candleholders sit on mismatched wooden tables. The aforementioned 'beautiful things' come in the form of artfully curated clothing, ceramics, textiles and jewellery and the wafting elegance of Cosmic Wonder's designer fashion. Books, coffee beans and more are all expertly chosen with an eye for the transcendent.

Their seasonal plant-based (vegan) lunches are made in limited quantities so book ahead online (stardustkyoto.com). Organic vegetables and grains are heroes in the changing savoury menu, each dish made with the utmost care and thought. Pair your lunch with an organic wine or whimsically presented seasonal fruit juice. Our favourite part of the meal is their seasonal 'raw' dessert presented on exquisite ceramics like tiny pieces of art adorned by little wisps of nature. Enjoy it while delightful host Kana floats in and out of the room radiating universal energy.

豆腐料理 空野 南船場店

TOFU RYORI SORANO MINAMISEMBA
OSAKA

4-5-6 Minamikyuhojimachi
Vertex Hommachi bldg
B1F, Chuo, Osaka

Honmachi station, then
walk (10min)

You'll find one of our favourite dining experiences in the basement of an architecturally designed building in the chic suburb of Osaka's Minamisemba. It's minimal yet intimate, a designer cave of light woods and crisp white walls with a soaring vaulted ceiling. Whether you sit at the bar gazing into the frenetic kitchen, or lounge in one of the cosy booths separated by creative screens, the atmosphere, low lights and the murmur of the crowd relaxes you.

Premium quality soybeans from Hokkaido are worked into various intriguing and delicious dishes. Tofu Ryori Sorano's creativity with tofu makes it a perfect vegetarian-friendly date night. Full of stylish locals, it's moderately priced for a memorable night out.

Delicious starters include avocado tofu or sesame tofu. The real drawcard is the tofu that forms at your table while you wait. A beautiful jewel box of curd is heated over a stone pot until it slowly transforms – you can't get tofu fresher than when you make it yourself. Carve it out with the wooden spatula provided and then drizzle with soy ... it would convert any tofu naysayer. Pair your dinner with the tofu or yuzu cocktail. For non-vegetarians there is also an array of excellent fish and meat dishes.

Be sure you leave room for their delicious desserts; Steve's favourite is the tofu tiramisu and Michelle's is the tofu cheesecake (sorry vegans, they contain milk). Tofu Ryori Sorano is a little pocket of calm in the rowdy and messy city that is Osaka.

ひょうたん温泉

HYOTAN ONSEN JIGOKU-MUSHI
BEPPU

The island of Kyushu is famous for its warm climate, warm hospitality and hot-spring water. The thermal activity creates hot-spring steam that spouts from the ground and it would be a waste not to cook with it.

Super onsen Hyotan features a jigoku-mushi, a rustic courtyard steam kitchen that serves noodles, eggs, seafood, chicken and tofu platters – all fresh Oita produce which you can steam yourself over bamboo baskets in stone ovens. Seafood sets are perfect for two and include crab, scallops, shrimp and fish. The tofu vegetable set is ideal for vegetarians, and a jigoku seafood pile is a mound of prawns, fish scallops and the coastal region's highly regarded crab. Don't forget to round your lunch off with a steamed custard pudding. Locals opt to bring their own ingredients, hiring a steam vent (charged by the half hour). You can also drink healing water direct from the source or inhale healing steam through a series of open pipes – it could help to loosen vocal cords if you're planning an evening of karaoke later on.

159-2 Kannawa
Beppu, Oita

hyotan-onsen.com

Beppu station, then
bus (25min)

民芸食事 寿々や

SUZUYA RESTAURANT
TAKAYAMA

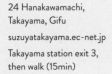

24 Hanakawamachi,
Takayama, Gifu

suzuyatakayama.ec-net.jp

Takayama station exit 3,
then walk (15min)

Surrounded by the Hida mountains deep in the Japanese Alps, Takayama's country attitude and location make for a perfect mini break. The Edo-period (1603 to 1867) town has a potent feudal history, which you absorb as you stroll through the narrow atmospheric streets lined with historic buildings.

Suzuya's folk architecture, reflecting the gassho farm houses the area is famous for, is an atmospheric mix of warm woods and light that diffuses gently through the narrow slat windows and shoji screens. We were seated in our own warm, cosy booth and the staff cared for us like we were locals. Two small clay grillers (hibachi) were brought to the table, each had a dried hoba (magnolia) leaf on top, housing an array of wild vegetables. The hoba miso paste, apparently a family recipe passed down through generations was mild, slightly sharp and sweet. Our lunch cooked itself at our table. Steve's hoba was a mix of mountain vegetables and the region's famed Hida beef, Michelle's hoba was adorned with colourful vegetables with an accent on mushrooms. Also on the menu is the luxe Hida beef sirloin, considered a melt-in-your-mouth sensation; and pescatarians will love the delicious deep-fried breaded prawns.

After the fortifying lunch you'll need a wander. Visit the town's specialty stores that include wood carving, excellent local sake, wagashi (Japanese sweets) and rice crackers, roasting and blistering on an open fire. If you are staying the night, the Miyagawa morning market showcases organic and farm-fresh produce.

農民カフェ

NOUMIN CAFE PROJECT
TOKYO

2-27-8 Kitazawa,
Setagaya, Tokyo

hyakushow.com/shimokitazawa

Shimokitazawa station west exit
Northside, then walk (5min)

Noumin Cafe (Farmer's Cafe) is a backstreet local that fits perfectly into Shimokita's 'every day is like Sunday' relaxed vintage vibe. The cafe exudes passion for food that is organically grown, freshly picked, earthy, natural and full of flavour; roots, shoots and legumes of all varieties are used in a delicious menu of seasonal organic fare. Housed in a rustic building in a quiet street, the exterior invites you in, warm and welcoming and augmented by a colourful farm-to-table mini market.

Inside, you can sit cross-legged at low tables or on a mishmash of retro furniture and cosy couches. In the small outside area, you can enjoy the fruits of a farmer's labours while looking at the Buddha statue and listening to the generated sounds of running water and the gentle plucking of koto strings.

Lunch set platters are seasonal, fresh, and unadorned. Veggie dishes feature a soup and a plate with a central mound of rice surrounded by crisp tempura and fresh tofu and salad and come with a side order of drinks and dessert. The lotus tea perfectly complements the nutritious food. Or you can choose from a plant-based curry and rice. Round it off with one of their delicious soy-based desserts washed down with an organic cocktail. If you prefer to sprawl out in a local park, their picturesque takeout window sells bento boxes, perfect for picnics.

うかい鳥山

3426 Minami Sakawa-machi,
Hachioji, Tokyo

Free shuttle from
Takaosanguchi station

UKAI TORIYAMA
MOUNT TAKAO

Mount Takao is only an hour from Tokyo but the mountainous ranges and forested glades will make you feel worlds away from the city. Ukai Toriyama is an experiential restaurant nested in a narrow valley girded by tall pines, replete with ponds, streams, bridges, statues and waterwheels, where butterflies flutter in hedges and insects buzz lazily in the undergrowth. The building style, sukiya-zukuri, is a classic form of Japanese residential architecture, once used for the tea ceremony and ikebana, designed with the pursuit of elegance in mind. Various private dining rooms are secreted about the verdant landscape, peering out from behind bright pink cherry blossoms or voluminous golden maple trees. Turning a corner, a moss-covered roof comes into view. Pods in subtle earth tones emerge unexpectedly from the undergrowth. Sitting in the rooms and gazing out over the landscape is half the experience.

Essentially a charcoal-grilled chicken restaurant, the set menus are seasonal and include a variety of chicken options, beef options and a kid's set menu. We visited at lunchtime and delighted in the feast of small plates and courses. Traditionally dressed waiters floated in and out of our private room bringing dish after dish of delicious food. Steve's lunch highlights included chicken and wagyu beef lightly grilled in Ukai's 'secret sauce', beautifully presented sashimi on a bed of rice augmented by floral arrangements, and the freshest locally sourced mountain vegetables. Michelle feasted on sashimi, somen noodles, tofu salad, barley rice and a delicious adzuki bean jelly for dessert. We returned another time at night to eat a feast while watching the sun go down and the fireflies dancing in the dark.

Booking online is essential (ukai.co.jp) and easy for English speakers.

近江町市場

50 Kamiomicho,
Kanazawa, Ishikawa

kanazawastation.com/
omicho-ichiba-market

Kanazawa station east side
bus to Musashigatsuji, then
walk (2min)

OMICHO ICHIBA MARKET
KANAZAWA

Famously known as 'the kitchen of Kanazawa', Omicho Ichiba Market (or
Omicho), has been supplying locals with fresh produce since 1721 CE! Over
200 lively market stalls cram into a grid of small, covered lanes not far from
Kanazawa station and the town's main attractions, Kenrokuen (*see* p. 156) and
the 21st-century Museum of Contemporary Art.

Local Kaga region delicacies on offer include the freshest of fruits and vegetables,
wagashi (Japanese sweets) and regional sake. The seafood is the star here
however, showcasing the bounty from the nearby Sea of Japan. Marvel at the
unusual food on offer and the tiny eating spaces serving plates crammed with
crab, yellowfin tuna, salmon and shrimp. Seafood bento boxes, fruit and delicious
mochi (sweet rice cake) make for a perfect picnic set.

Prop yourself up at one of the freshly shucked oyster bars with an Oriental
Brewing craft beer and watch the flurry of shoppers go by. Our favourite
market meal is Kanazawa's renowned kaisendon – a delicious melt-in-your-
mouth sashimi bowl on a bed of sweet rice. Michelle always orders the tuna
bowl, Steve's favourite is the salmon. The region's famous gold leaf ornaments
your humble rice bowl, giving it a luxe Kanazawa twist. There are plenty of tiny
kaisendon eateries amongst the ramshackle stalls.

It's a tradition of ours to visit early on our first day. Watching the locals and
restaurant owners weave in and out of the stores to the sounds of the stall
owners hawking their produce is an inspiring start to the day. At lunchtime,
join a line and prepare for a locally sourced, fresh and delicious meal.

Mindful
sleeping

Our favourite memories of Japanese travel always include the places we've stayed. Japan is full of otherworldly overnight experiences, from the eco-friendly or luxe to the highly unusual. We never fail to be delighted, surprised and often deeply moved by the hospitality, locations, views, hot-spring baths and incredible food. From spiritually enriching temple stays (see p. 133) to time-honoured ryokan (traditional Japanese inn) with onsen (see p. 57), off-the-grid sustainable lodgings that love the environment and are loved back, and forested mountain retreats, Japan is a treasure-trove of considered and elevated accommodation.

One experience you should not miss is staying in a ryokan. The oldest recorded ryokan are Nishiyama Onsen Keiunkan in Hayakawa (705 CE), recognised as the oldest hotel in the world, and Hoshi Ryokan in Komatsu (718 CE). Designed as rest stops for weary samurai and merchants, their sole purpose is to provide hospitality, regional cooking, a relaxing environment, a bath (usually hot springs) and a cosy night's sleep. Prices can seem high but considering your meals are included and the amenities can be numerous and high quality, it is money well spent. Ryokan will often be in older cities, small towns or amongst spectacular nature.

Most special stays will greet you with tea and wagashi (Japanese sweets). You may be taken on a mini tour to show you the public spaces, which may include baths, cosy libraries and reading nooks, ikebana (flower displays) and amazing arts and crafts. Some accommodation will include a mini shop selling local wares and their signature pyjamas, yukata (summer cotton kimono) and towels. We highly recommend booking a Japanese breakfast for at least one morning of your stay. Fish, rice, egg and vegetable dishes with unlimited green tea will set you up for your day's adventures.

In this chapter, we've curated a mini list of our favourite overnight stays. Try a traditional Japanese farmhouse stay where you can become one with the cycle of life in a rural setting and where food is sourced directly from the land. Sleep amidst a field of artworks and turn into your own installation. Become a fearless (and highly pampered) adventurer as you settle down for the night in a fully equipped yurt. Sleep with the birds in a contemporary, eco-friendly treehouse. Partake in the ultimate glamping experience, hugged by nature, without giving up any of your creature comforts.

Wherever you stay, buy some bath salts, a face mask and some pampering products (we always buy foot cream) and have at least one cosy night in. Turn off your tech, make time for a long bath, some meditation and some haiku poetry and take care of your whole self.

Previous: Kishi-Kei; *top:* Steve sleeping on tatami floors in a ryokan; *opposite top left:* HOSHINOYA Fuji; *opposite top right:* Hatcho No Yu; *opposite bottom:* Treeful Treehouse

ホテルウッド

80-2 Kamininomachi,
Takayama, Gifu

hotel-wood.com

Takayama station, then
taxi (5min) or walk

HOTEL WOOD
TAKAYAMA

In the historic township of Takayama, Hotel Wood uses the key principles
of Zen as its core objective to deliver a mindful stay dedicated to the gentle
art of relaxation. The first thing you'll notice is the architecture which makes
extensive and innovative use of the wood from the area's plentiful yew trees.
It's a contemporary and clever take on classic Takayama architecture that blends
in perfectly with the dark, detailed wood of the traditional surrounds. Furniture in
the hotel is by local craftspeople and simply appointed rooms with shoji screens
and diffused light blend the very best of Japanese aesthetics with Western-style
comforts, including a wheelchair-friendly (barrier-free) space.

Hotel Wood prides itself on the kind of omotenashi (hospitality) experienced in
days gone by, when the world moved at a slower pace. On arrival, relax with a
whisked matcha under the vast wooden canopy in the shared space, which will
set the tone for your stay. Shared spaces in the hotel include a photo gallery, the
Zen room with its three-quarter moon-shaped window and a large public bath.

Hotel Wood has an extensive itinerary for anyone wanting to involve themselves
in the mindful experiences of the Takayama region. Some are free and some
charge a small fee. Take an atmospheric night tour of the old town, or book in
advance for a matcha tea experience. Take advantage of the extremely mindful
seven sake tastings. The guided walking tour and meditation session at stunning
Zennoji temple is a must-do. Nearby Shiroyama Park is ranked in the top
100 therapeutic forest walks, and if you visit in spring there are over 1000 sakura
(cherry blossom) trees, and Hotel Wood offers an early morning walk (2hr) which
includes a breakfast bento box. If you feel like a whole day trek, sign up for the
guided tour of Hida-Osaka Falls, which includes a tour of the lava plateau forests
that are sometimes carpeted by a blanket of fallen leaves. Book online (hotel-
wood.com) five days in advance.

岸家

21-5 Sakanoshita,
Kamakura, Kanagawa

kishi-ke.co.jp

Kamakura station,
then taxi (5min)

KISHI-KE MODERN RYOKAN
KAMAKURA

A contemporary take on a traditional ryokan (traditional Japanese inn), Kishi-ke's experiential stay in Kamakura is luxe, boutique and perfect for a honeymoon or special occasion. Kamakura is not far from Tokyo, but feels worlds away. Its many temples include Kotokuin which features the large, iconic 'Great Buddha' (1252 CE); the hydrangea temple Meigetsuin (1394 CE), with its impressive circular window's autumnal view; and Hasedera (736 CE).

Kishi-ke's Kanji consists of two words: travel and building – in short, they see themselves as 'a home away from home'. There's another word linked to this wondrous space, the Zen concept of chisoku: to be 'fulfilled within the here and now'. Hosts CEO Nobuyuki Kishi, a descendant of an Okayama samurai family, and art director Hitomi Kishi, a mistress of the tea ceremony, will help bring stillness and contentment to your everyday life.

The immaculate space, designed by Kengo Kuma disciple Ryohei Tanaka, has ocean views and overlooks a beautiful landscape garden, designed by Akihiko Ono. Beautifully considered rooms have a palette of pale wood, white and deep grey. Bathrooms include a mini onsen and a hinoki wooden bath with handmade medicinal bath salts. Your room's ceramics, vases and tools are made by local artisans and appreciate wabi-sabi, the art of perfection in imperfection, a concept harmonious with chisoku.

Dining includes exquisite seasonal, plant-based shojin ryori, a luxe update on Buddhist cuisine, and health-conscious spins on classic Japanese dishes. Kishi-ke also offer a variety of experiences (both free and for an extra fee), including mindful zazen meditation, ikebana, the tea ceremony and wind surfing (Nobuyuki Kishi was a keen windsurfer in his school days). Write this place into your itinerary – and then start counting down the days.

紅葉館

KOYOKAN RYOKAN
YASUGI

528 Kiyomizu-cho,
Yasugi, Shimane

kouyoukan.co.jp

Yasugi station, then shuttle bus

MINDFUL TIP

Make it a special all-round experience and catch the Sunrise Izumo train from Tokyo, the last remaining overnight train in Japan. Take your time getting there and you'll be in the right frame of mind when you arrive.

Shimane's country hospitality began for us when Koyokan sent a shuttle bus to Yasugi station to carry us into the arms of the forest. We were taken high into the mountains, reaching a steeply sloped road that afforded stunning views of the Zuikozan, the pagoda of Kiyomizudera temple, majestic as it soared over the sea of lush treetops.

The temple complex belongs to the Tendai sect and dates back to 1429 CE. Pilgrims come for 'Yakubarai', a special prayer ceremony for the reversal of bad fortune. The three-tiered pagoda is the only one in Japan where visitors can explore the third level, and the Hozo treasure house features the region's largest Buddha statue.

Koyokan sits at the base of the temple, once a teahouse for pilgrims in the late Edo period (1603 to 1867), now an atmospheric ryokan (traditional Japanese inn). A meandering path led us from the temple grounds. We inspected mosses and lichens of all varieties along the way and pondered in revered tones about the potential age of the towering trees. Reaching the ryokan, we saw that Michelle's name was inscribed on a wooden plaque on the door in Kanji, a respectful welcome and a marker of old-world hospitality. Our spacious room was decorated with ornate wooden eaves and alcoves displaying objects celebrating the region's history. We took tea in our own glassed-off corridor, overlooking lush nature, the sweet scent of tatami mingling with melodious birdsong.

Dinner is Buddhist temple food at its best, humble and agrarian, yet lavish and detailed. Mostly vegetarian, expect rice and miso paired with seasonal, locally sourced vegetable dishes, pickles and artful creations with roots, stems and leaves.

Staying within metres of the temple grounds is a special experience. During the day wander around the spectacular and ancient buildings. At dusk a contemplative silence descends.

星のや富士

1408 Oishi, Fujikawaguchiko-
machi, Minamitsuru-gun,
Yamanashi

hoshinoya.com/fuji/en

Kawaguchiko station, then
taxi (18min)

HOSHINOYA FUJI GLAMPING
KAWAGUCHIKO

They say it's not the destination but the journey, but HOSHINOYA Fuji begs
to differ. A side-trip from frenetic Tokyo, HOSHINOYA has created a glamp-
ground escape in the mountains of Yamanashi gazing over resplendent Lake
Kawaguchiko with a visual crescendo of awe-inspiring Mount Fuji. This is no
log cabin in the woods, starting a fire with two sticks and fighting off a bear
experience. It is an arresting architectural forest resort, an artful blend of nature
and nurture provided by the masters of experiential Japanese accommodation.

HOSHINOYA makes you feel that you are at one with, but not at the mercy
of, nature. A cluster of minimalist 'cabin' boxes with large balconies jut out of
a verdant mountainside. Interiors have giant glass windows that act as a living
artwork for the incomparable vistas. Cabin choices include king, double and an
option to include three people and all have sweeping views of mountains. Your
friends are the surrounding red pines, cherry, ginkgo and maple trees (a world
of vibrant colour in all seasons).

The hunter-gatherer food concept here gives you three eating choices. Local
farmers provide fresh fruits and vegetables or for meat enthusiasts, local hunters
deliver wild deer and boar. The dining hall offers French-inspired food. Or DIY
dining outdoors in the forest kitchen with the help of the resident glamping
master. For an intimate night in, have your food brought to your pod.

Take the Fujisan panoramic view mountain trek. What could be more mindful
than gazing out onto one of the world's most impressive and spiritual mountains
as it looms majestically over mirror-still Lake Kawaguchiko? Guests can also
participate in food smoking, canoeing, nature tours, and aerial body stretch
classes. This is camping HOSHINOYA style – immersed in nature, relaxing
and isolated while never feeling that you have strayed too far from your
creature comforts.

ツリーフルツリーハウス

2578 Genka, Nago
Okinawa

treeful.net

Haneda Airport to Naha
Airport, hire a car to Nago

TREEFUL TREEHOUSE SUSTAINABLE RESORT
NAGO, OKINAWA

Become a 'morinchu' ('forest person' in Okinawan) and climb your way to a more sustainable accommodation experience. Treeful Treehouse is 30 minutes by car from the closest town and is situated in the middle of the Nago Forest, a resort where you can live out the childhood fantasy of staying the night high in a treehouse, while not giving up your status as an adult. Different styles and sizes of treehouses dot the verdant canopy of the northern Okinawan Forest. It's a carefully executed nature resort where every part honours the environment and utilises local growers and makers. It eschews the use of fossil fuels, has a compostable toilet, uses solar energy and rainwater tanks and a local well provides natural mineral water to guests.

Feeling at one with nature is easy, the treehouses are open on all sides giving you a 360-degree view of the treetops, gently swaying in the breeze, and at night aglow with the shimmer of lightning bugs. The sound of the river and the natural world lulls you to sleep. The Floating DNA Catwalk is a space in the trees for wellness practices like yoga and meditation. Imagine saluting the sun when you are just that little bit closer to it. The Catwalk also acts as a ramp, providing wheelchair access. A communal 'Aerohouse' features a bathroom, relaxation rooms and a kitchen.

As Treeful's location is remote, you'll need to think about eating options. You can bring your own food, choose a box of locally sourced produce to be cooked on the communal fire-pit or select dinner prepared by a local chef using the island's famous organic ingredients. Email the caring staff in advance for plant-based or allergy dietary requests. Treeful also offer a rugged trekking tour for an extra fee. Guide Kijimuna Yasu will load you into her eight-wheel vehicle and take you through the forest to the sea (where, if you're lucky, you can catch a glimpse of sea turtles). A lunch pit stop with a delicious bento box and a swim at Shizogumui waterfall are all part of the package.

八寿恵荘

4098 Hirotsu, Ikeda
Kitaazumi district, Nagano

yasuesou.com

Akashina station, then shuttle
car or taxi (30min)

YASUESOU BIO HOTEL
IKEDA

Situated in the Japanese Alps, Nagano prefecture is known for its hot-spring water and arresting nature. After a mini-break visiting the Matsumoto craft fair, we decided to go rural and spend the night at nearby nature-stay hotel Yasuesou – a perfect, mindful escape for calm moments, country walks and flower fields.

Yasuesou is a modern chalet-style hotel in the southern alps, surrounded by sprawling fields of chamomile flowers and was the first organic hotel to open in Japan. Its emphasis on healing supports guests with a wide variety of ailments, using relaxation, yoga and pure food.

Their commitment to the environment shines through in every aspect of the sustainable hotel's design. Nagano prefectural woods were used to build the hotel – and the scent of cedar, red pine, ash, cherry and chestnut gives the already impressive visual feast a powerful olfactory presence. The minimalist modern Japanese interior of pale wood will have you snapping shots of your room to take home to re-create the style and mood. You can relax in the communal library space or head outside and climb their purpose-built treehouse and take in the views of the Hida mountain ranges.

The Kamitsuren No Yu is a hot-springs bath where the chamomile suffuses the water, promoting total relaxation. Soak in the bath while gazing through giant windows that overlook the forests that clothe the Hida mountains. The flowers are also used to produce shampoo and body care products under their own brand, Kamitsuren. Buy some products to take home to recreate the Kamitsuren No Yu experience.

At mealtimes all food is organic and includes vegetarian options, locally sourced, foraged and carefully prepared mountain vegetables free from chemical additives or harsh seasonings. As they say at Yasuesou, 'Taste the blessings of the earth'.

民宿かんじゃ

MINSHUKU KANJA
SHIRAKAWAGO

Shirakawago and Gokayama are small villages known for their striking gassho-zukuri farmhouses (a triangular sloped-roof style known as 'praying hands' – slotted together without the use of nails, which, even now, are used to house silkworms), many whose origins go back 250 years. Looking like the gingerbread houses on biscuit tin lids, these cottage-style abodes are wooden with white-panelled walls. The rooftops were made to withstand snow, an impressive architectural feat and one which allows for some nursery rhyme vistas in winter, especially, as we discovered, when lit up at night.

Ogimachi village in Shirakawago has the largest collection of gassho-zukuri. When we strolled through the village in winter, snow slipping dangerously off the angled roofs, dried persimmon hanging in clusters from the eaves, it made us feel like we were characters in our own fairytale.

An array of gassho-zukuri are set up as accommodation, offering travellers the unique experience of staying in a traditional Japanese farmhouse. We chose Kanja for its location, perched upon a hilltop and overlooking the village, taking in a view of Myozenji temple, a gassho-style temple and museum.

Kanja has five guest rooms and a large communal dining hall. The hall features a Japanese-style hearth where dishes are made using fresh local produce. They are mostly vegetarian farm-to-table meals. Rooms are large and cater for four or more people and bathroom facilities are shared. Wi-fi will likely be non-existent, so just enjoy traditional Japanese rustic life off the grid.

689 Ogimachi, Shirakawa-mura, Ono-gun, Gifu

en.sirakawago-kanjiya.com

Takayama station Nohi bus to Shirakawago bus stop, then walk (5min)

MINDFUL TIP

Minshuku roughly translates as bed and breakfast. Book through the wonderful website: japaneseguesthouses.com.

八丁湯

876 Kawamata, Nikko, Tochigi
Free shuttle from Meotobuchi
parking

HATCHO NO YU RYOKAN
OKUKINU ONSEN, NIKKO

A mindful trip doesn't get more authentic than a visit to Okukinu onsen, a hidden hot spring in the middle of the vast lush Nikko forests and mountains. Okukino brims with character (and hot-spring water) with the town's four ryokan (traditional Japanese inns) opening up for day-bathing experiences.

Making a pilgrimage to this quiet pocket of Japan will not disappoint those who seek quiet contemplation and arresting nature. Hatcho no yu, or the Inn of the Hidden Springs, sits at an altitude of 1300 metres (4265 feet), where proliferous nature, rocky outcrops and stunning vistas abound. Known as 'Lodge of the Lamps', various lamps light the way, harking back to the days when there was no power deep in the forest – a not-too-distant 1988. Choose from two types of room: traditional Japanese or spacious log cabins, as well as 'barrier free' rooms for guests with disabilities, many which suit families or large groups. Some have loft-style sleeping and all offer views that perfectly frame nature.

The hiking and autumn foliage are spectacular, but without doubt the highlight is the range of hot springs. Most are mixed gender, and several have a view of a rare 'hot' waterfall, where spring water steams as it cascades down the rocks. The baths include Takimi no yu, (the bath of waterfall viewing), Yukimi no yu (the bath of snow viewing) and Shakunage no yu (the bath of rhododendron), a mixed bath that also overlooks the waterfall. You can choose from same-sex baths and there are women-only times for mixed baths.

The food also impresses, with platters of the freshest sashimi and vegetable dishes locally sourced from the abundance of the mountain. Hunter-gatherer types may like to partake in freshly hunted deer and wild boar. Hatcho no yu is deep in wild forest, truly one of Japan's best-kept secrets.

農家民宿 フォレスト

FOREST
WAJIMA, NOTO PENINSULA

6-31-1 Wada,
Monzen-machi, Wajima

notoforest.com

Anamizu station, then
hotel shuttle (on request)

Branching off from Honshu's mid-west, Noto peninsula has rugged coastlines with stunning scenery, fertile soil, thick forests and a sunset like no other. The area is prone to seasonal extremes, which it uses in its favour. Thick snow melts into mineral-rich water. Thunderous seas counterpoint relaxing hot-spring baths and provide Noto with fresh seafood. You'll also find Soji here, the head temple of the Soto sect of Buddhism.

Forest at Noto Peninsula accept booking for only one group at a time, allowing you and your travelling partners the perfect chance for a city circuit-breaker. The beautiful building is rural and rustic, giving you a sense of being at one with the land.

Forest offer a three-day and two-night package which focuses on a deep understanding of Noto's landscape, unique culture, characters and specialties. Activities include hiking the forested glades while picking local wildflowers, and exploring nearby wonders with Noto locals as your guides. You can visit local craft shops (lacquerware is renowned in Noto) or do a craft workshop, such as making your own Japanese paper.

The carefully prepared organic food is a highlight at Forest. Breakfast and dinner use locally sourced produce which is transformed into a feast for the eyes and the senses. In an area famous for its sake and craft beers, a curated list is on offer to complement your evening meal.

MINDFUL TIP
Take some time out from all the activities to shed your cares (and clothes) at famous health resort Wakura Onsen, just 40 minutes away.

光の館

2891 Ueno-Ko,
Tokamachi, Niigata

hikarinoyakata.com

Hokuhoku line from Echigo-
Yuzawa station (Tokyo) to
Tokamachi, then taxi (15min)

ECHIGO TSUMARI HOUSE OF LIGHT
TOKAMACHI, NIIGATA

The Echigo Tsumari Art Field is an open-air art exhibition spread over six spaces
in Tokamachi. Exhibitions are both permanent and temporary with the Echigo
Tsumari Triennial an unmissable event for all art lovers. Unusually, you can stay
the night in various artworks.

American Light and Space Movement artist James Turrell was given the brief
to create a guest house that also functioned as a meditation space, inspired by
Michelle's favourite essay, Jun'ichirō Tanizaki's *In Praise of Shadows*. *The House
of Light* resembles a traditional Japanese house. However, where a house would
let light in, the House of Light uses interior light to contrast with external
light. At night it resembles a lantern aglow like a firefly perched defiantly in
enveloping darkness. A lightshow creates various atmospheres through cycles
of gentle change.

Inside, you can meditate in the 'Cloister' and observe the changing seasons.
During the day, the power of the sun pours in through a skylight in the 'Outside-
in' room. The 'Light bath' has fibre optics that illuminate the depths of the water,
allowing you to see every detail of the bath and its inhabitants. The full-length
windows in the 'Room of Gardens' bring the guest closer to the natural world.

Sleeping inside your own artwork, not just as an observer, but as an aspect of the
art is a memorable experience. Turrell's desire was for three families or groups to
stay at the artwork and to share their emotions and insights. Reasonably priced
delicious dinners can be catered for on request, or cook up your own feast in
the kitchen.

心を満たす寺院滞在

Mindful
temple
stays

MINDFUL TIPS

Shukubo (temple lodgings) are an integral part of pilgrimage trails. Major temples can have shukubo inside the temple grounds or scattered around the vicinity. They can vary widely, some may have curfews and set activities, others may feel more like you are staying in a ryokan (traditional Japanese inn).

The suffixes 'ji' and 'dera' mean 'temple'.

Japan has an estimated 80,000 Buddhist temples, and many act as peaceful meditation retreats. From mountainous hideaways and secretive forest compounds to serene escapes near major city hubs, some of our most life-affirming experiences in Japan have been overnight stays at Buddhist temples. So, turn off your tech, prepare for a holiday from your usual self and submit to the life of a monk, limiting your spoken word, eating cleanly and spending time in quiet meditation.

As the Japanese proverb says: 'In Zen we don't find the answers, we lose the questions'. Taking this kind of break clears the mind and purifies the heart. Be respectful and dress modestly and remember you are staying in a working religious community. 'Be a witness to your own thoughts' (another Zen proverb) and submit to a life-changing experience that will empower you with rituals you can take home and use in your everyday life.

Shukubo lodgings (the name can be translated as 'sleeping with the monks) are the perfect way to experience the full scope of life in and around temples and pilgrimage trails. Accommodation is almost always traditional Japanese rooms with tatami mats, futons and shared amenities. Rooms often eschew the distractions of modern life like televisions and internet (although you will usually find yourself not far from a wi-fi connection). Your experience will include all aspects of temple life, from early morning prayers and meditation to dawn and dusk gongs, chanting, hot-springs bathing, calligraphy lessons, tea ceremonies and shojin ryori (vegetarian banquets) made with locally sourced produce. The noise of the city will quickly recede as you enter unforgettable garden grounds, meditate within spectacular ancient buildings while gazing over impressive landscapes and immerse yourself in the traditions and practices of Buddhist doctrine.

Previous: Shunkoin Temple; *opposite top left:* Kakurinbo Shukubo; *opposite top right and bottom:* Chionin Temple

春光院

42 Hanazonomyoshinjicho,
Ukyo-ku, Kyoto

shunkoin.com/en

Hanazono station,
then walk (10min)

SHUNKOIN TEMPLE

KYOTO

Shunkoin is a sub-temple of the Myoshinji compound (Temple of the Excellent Mind – the largest school of Rinzai). Dating back over 400 years, the temple's atmospheric dark wooden structures are offset perfectly against the surrounding trees. The garden's azaleas were planted by famed Buddhist lecturer D.T. Suzuki (*see p. 36*). Spiritual leader Rev. Takafumi Zenryu Kawakami's main objective is to teach meditation, philosophy, and wellbeing to all visitors. His commitment to sharing Zen has seen him guest lecture around the world, sharing his deep knowledge on mindfulness.

Shunkoin offer stays at Tetsuryu-Kutsu, their modern guest house. Their cosy Japanese-style rooms with private bathrooms include free bicycle rental so you can ride to incredible nearby landmarks, like Arashiyama, Ryoanji, Kinkakuji or Nijo Castle. There are also one- to three-day Zen meditation retreats scheduled throughout the year. Book or enquire online (shunkoin.com).

Zen Buddhism teaches observance, calmness, awareness and connection. These pillars are intrinsically entwined with three mindful practices with origins in Zen, which Shunkoin offer classes in. Zazen (meditation) is taught, in English, in the magnificent prayer hall featuring Kano Eigaku gold leaf screen paintings. A private tea ceremony, calligraphy and koto classes are also available, and for those who cannot travel they also host classes online.

Shunkoin is one of the rare Zen temples that perform same-sex marriages. Their philosophy is this: 'We believe all love is equal and are open to all types of couples'. The wedding includes the chanting of the heart sutra and the sake-sharing ritual and is available in English ... worth travelling for.

知恩院和順会館

400-2 Rinkacho,
Higashiyama-ku, Kyoto

wajun-kaikan.jp

Higashiyama station,
then walk (10min)

CHIONIN WAJUN-KAIKAN
KYOTO

In a temple compound within easy reach of Gion-dori, Chionin, the head temple of the Jodoshu (Pure Land) sect of Buddhism, has origins spreading back to 1175 CE. The existing main gate (the largest wooden gate in Japan) and the Sutra repository date back to 1633. The grounds are famous for their autumn colour and sakura (cherry blossom) trees.

Walking around Chionin is an adventure. It features 'seven wonders', including the nightingale hall (an early form of burglar alarm where floorboards squeak to alert you to intruders); the 'forgotten umbrella', reputedly left behind by a grateful fox; and the Sanpō Shōmen Mamuki-no-Neko, a picture of a cat that can see in three directions – scour the grounds on a treasure hunt.

Chionin Wajun-Kaikan is a contemporary shukubo (temple lodging) that has the appearance of a modernist hotel. Designed in 2011 by the Takenaka Corporation, the Zen aesthetic of the architecture sits neatly next to ancient Chionin temple. A choice of Japanese or Western rooms is available (we always choose Japanese). Gorgeous communal bathing facilities will cleanse your mind and body. Packages include a shojin ryori (vegetarian banquet) dinner and breakfast at Kasuian restaurant. Wi-fi is available in all rooms and their onsite coffee shop will revive your spirits. The temple holds classes in meditation, calligraphy and tours in English.

総持院

143 Koyasan, Ito-gun,
Wakayama
Gokurakubashi station, then
cable car, then bus (20min)

SOUJIIN TEMPLE
MOUNT KOYA

We made the pilgrimage to Koyasan (Mount Koya) one icy winter to learn
more about, and stay with, the monks of the Shingon Buddhist sect. For over
1000 years this sacred mountain has been their home, not far from Osaka and
yet miles away from that city's frenetic energy. Soujiin was our choice from over
50 shokubo (temple lodgings) on the mountain.

Soujiin is a working Heian-period (794 to 1185 CE) monastery. Staying here
is a complete experience, taking in meditation, onsen, shojin ryori (vegetarian
banquet) dinner and breakfast. We slipped off our shoes and our host walked us
through eerie corridors of well-polished wood punctuated by crane murals and
objects of religious significance. Our room was a classic Japanese guest room
complete with scented tatami, warm woods, delightful katomado (flower windows)
and decorative fusuma (sliding panels), some which feature artworks dating
back centuries.

Like us, you'll be keen to get into the hot-springs bath, then head to dinner –
a memorable shojin ryori plant-based banquet with small plates of impressively
sculptured fresh local produce, beautifully made and skilfully arranged. At 6am
we joined the morning meditation and prayer session. As we sat in silence in the
ornate hall observing the monks' rituals, swathed in wisps of incense, we knew it
was something we'd carry with us always.

Koyasan's importance cannot be underestimated – it is both the start and the end
point of the famed Shikoku 88 Temple Pilgrimage (see p. 190). Minimal English
is spoken, adding to the authenticity of the experience, so switch off, unwind and
add your own meditations to centuries of holy contemplation.

鹿苑寺

24 Sagakitabori-cho,
Ukyo-ku, Kyoto

Randen-saga station,
then walk (8min)

ROKUOIN TEMPLE
ARASHIYAMA

Secretly spectacular, Rinzai Zen Buddhist temple Rokuoin is one of our favourite places to visit in autumn. With a history dating back to 1380 CE, it's known for its main path, flanked by maple trees, making for a mindful stroll in the early autumn when the leaves turn into blazing russets and golds. The long, dreamy stone path to the temple should be walked slowly, reflecting on the clipped hedges and visible tangled roots from ancient trees along the way. The Zen proverb 'Do not speak. Unless it improves on silence', is our mantra here.

On the grounds is a small, inexpensive shukubo (temple lodging) that caters to women only (men can visit the temple, but not stay). Sleep like the monks did centuries ago in one of their seven Japanese-style rooms with shoji screens, tatami and futons. Turn off your tech and embrace the moment. There are morning sermons and prayers and zazen (meditation) sessions are held later in the afternoon. A shojin ryori (vegetarian banquet) breakfast is included and all facilities, including bathing, are communal. It's old-world in every way, including a 7.30pm curfew. Participation in the aesthetic practices are expected. Bookings are by telephone in Japanese only, so ask a Japanese friend or other accommodation to telephone ahead and book for you. This is a very honest Japanese experience, with the reward of wonderful autumn foliage, for the she/her set who want to get away from the crowds.

大本山永平寺

5-15 Shihi, Eiheji,
Yoshida, Fukui

daihonzan-eiheiji.com

Fukui station bus to Eiheiji
(30min)

DAIHONZAN EIHEIJI TEMPLE

FUKUI

One of the two head temples of the Soto sect, Eiheiji (Temple of Eternal Wisdom), dates back to a staggering 1244 CE. Accessible from nearby Fukui city and a perfect daytrip from Kyoto, the temple is an astounding wooden complex, with many of the 70 buildings adjoined by canopied walkways. Overlooked by Mount Atago and girded by a micro forest of ancient, looming cedars, the grounds are complemented by the changing seasons. With a soundtrack of nature and tolling bells, a feeling of calm washes over you as you silently trek the paths of the Zen Buddhist monks.

An overnight stay at Eiheiji is otherworldly. Immerse yourself in the temple's deep history, admiring the large bronze temple bell, made in 1327 CE, and the Joyoden (founders hall) where the ashes of past masters are given platters of food daily – a powerful symbol of the endurance of their teachings. There are 100 monks that still serve here today, who still practise shikantaza or 'single-minded sitting', which was created by the first Zen master of Eiheiji, Dogen.

Sleep in a traditional Japanese room (shared bathrooms), eat shojin ryori (vegetarian banquet) and practise meditation with the monks. A more contemporary option is the temple's new Hakujukan Hotel in the adjacent 'Zen Village', which is overseen by Eiheiji temple staff who act as 'Zen concierges'. Stunning rooms exhibit a modern architectural take on Zen (and feature ensuites if sharing doesn't appeal to you). Relax in the Zen library, practise meditation or steep in the onsen (hot springs) 'Kosuikai'. Restaurant Suisen is immaculate and offers unforgettable vegetarian and regional cuisine meals. If you prefer, immerse yourself in experiences at the temple, knowing that you have a luxurious room to go back to.

覚林坊

3510 Minobu,
Minobu-cho,
Minamikoma-gun,
Yamanashi

kakurinbo.com

Minobu station, then bus to
Minobusan, then walk (10min)

KAKURINBO SHUKUBO

YAMANASHI

Cradled at the foothills of Mount Fuji, Kakurinbo resides in Gyogakuin
sub-temple in the grounds of Kuonji Temple on land that has been home to
the Nichiren Shu sect of Buddhism since the late 1200s.

From the time you arrive to the time you leave, the level of service at Kakurinbo
is exemplary. Historic rooms with wooden ceilings and delicately painted screens
are magical in the half light of the afternoon or early morning. Kakurinbo
specialises in kaiseki banquets that feature yuba (tofu skin) and fresh local
vegetables that will make you rethink your regular diet, all served on beautiful
ceramics and lacquerware and with their popular Kakurinbo temple beer. Wine
from the nearby Koshu Wine Valley can be enjoyed on the Sakurajisu terrace.

Early morning prayers will clear your mind and help you ponder the deep beauty
of the temple grounds which include a famous garden (with koi pond) designed
by poet and Zen master Muso Kokushi in the early 1300s. Yoga and sutra copying
can be enjoyed surrounded by nature. For those perfect photographs in the
beautiful grounds, Kakurinbo dress you in formal kimono. Café Zencho make
memorable and spectacular meals using local ingredients. The temple's omiyage
(souvenirs) include Nito-chan tea (honeysuckle, matcha and chrysanthemum)
and miracle Minobu water eye-drops.

Kakurinbo provide e-bikes to help you get around. Nearby 13th-century Kuonji
(eternity temple), is reached by climbing 287 steps (lucky you had that fortifying
traditional Japanese breakfast). The climb rewards you with a spectacular five-
tiered pagoda and temple bell and views of Minobusan village below. The village
specialises in paper and fireworks making, calligraphy and pottery.

MINDFUL TIP

Don't miss nearby Lake
Motosu (40min drive), which
presents the famed view of
Fujisan that features on the
¥1000 note.

大進坊宿坊

Toge-95, Haguromachi,
Tsuruoka, Yamagata

Yamagata station to
Tsuruoka station, then
bus to Mount Haguro

DAISHINBO SHUKUBO
TSURUOKA, YAMAGATA

The sacred area of the Dewa Sanzan is dotted with temples and places of religious significance and, owing to the regular pilgrims, there are many shukubo (both temple and pilgrim lodgings) scattered about the area. Their popularity in the Edo period (1603 to 1867 CE) boomed with three million Japanese pilgrims on their own spiritual quests. Back then the area was home to 300 lodgings, but today only 30 remain.

Resting on the grounds of the Sankoin temple, Daishinbo is a rustic and honest shukubo at the base of the sacred mountains (Mount Haguro is only a 10-minute drive away) and near the famed five-tiered pagoda, which is spectacular when lit up at night. You'll be sleeping like an Edo-period traveller did some 350 years ago, gazing out onto the same perfectly clipped trees and soaking in the same communal baths.

Kind and generous English-speaking staff will take the very best care of you throughout your stay. Expect futons on tatami mats, early morning prayers and an intensely traditional experience. Wi-fi is available just in case you feel like reconnecting with the world outside. Make sure to brave the steep stone steps up nearby Mount Gassan ('Moon Mountain', so named because of its resemblance to the moon when covered in snow), where you will find memorable views of mountaintops peeking shyly above cottony clouds. The shukubo on the Dewa Sanzan has perfected its own version of a shojin ryori (vegetarian banquet), including food in five colours and a delicious sesame tofu.

善光寺 淵之坊

ZENKOJI FUCHINOBO SHUKUBO
NAGANO

462 Nagano, Motoyoshicho,
Nagano

zenkoji.jp

Nagano station, then
bus or walk (30min)

Nagano grew organically around Zenkoji (Temple of Benevolent Light), which dates to the 7th century CE, before Buddhism. The temple holds the distinction of (secretly) housing the first statue of the Buddha to arrive in Japan. So important is the statue that only a replica is available for viewing on rare occasions (once every six years in spring) and even this replica is treated with great reverence. Visit the main hall, regarded as a National Treasure, then head down to the basement where, in total darkness, you can search for the 'key to paradise' – a literal key attached to the wall which will grant you salvation upon contact. The stunning Sutra repository (1759 CE) houses the sutra holder (1694 CE), which you can rotate to gain enlightenment.

You'll find a contemporary shukubo lodging at Zenkoji Fuchinobo Shukubo (1985) in the temple grounds. A choice of Western- or Japanese-style rooms is available, all with shared facilities. A communal bath is perfect to steep in after sunrise prayers. The lodging is famous for its shojin ryori (vegetarian banquet), which uses fresh local ingredients and is served in a sumptuous communal hall.

Purchase a ticket to the inner sanctuary and attend the morning service (O-Asaji) which starts according to the sunrise. Michelle loved the monk's incredible attire and the giant gold hanging lanterns. On request they will organise a special prayer service for your lost loved one, a moving and cathartic experience.

別府禅リトリート

BEPPU ZEN RETREAT
OITA

3462-4 Toyooka,
Hiji, Hayami-gun, Oita

beppuzenretreat.com

Beppu station to Bungo
Toyooka station, then
walk (15min)

Beppu is a favourite Kyushu destination of ours, an onsen town famous for its fiery 'hells' – hot-spring sources that steam, billow, huff and puff and spout as they make their way to the surface. Relaxing onsen dot the winding streets and lanes of the town and countryside making it a breezy place to let yourself unwind. Adding the calming Beppu Zen Retreat to your Kyushu itinerary will help you sink deeply into nature and let your stresses and cares float away with the clouds of steam that rise up from the Beppu Hells.

Beppu Zen Retreat is held in Gyateiji, a Rinzai Zen temple dating back to 1346 CE, flanked by mountains on one side and an enticing sea view on the other. For three generations the temple has belonged to the Kodo family. Once a physics teacher, Zen monk Yodo Kono now devotes his life to Zen practice. Referred to lovingly as a mix between a temple stay and a home stay, the retreat is a family affair. Kono's wife teaches calligraphy and his mother has an impressive 45 years of experience in the tea ceremony. Meals often involve your participation, so add cooking classes to your agenda.

Onsite zazen (meditation) will teach you a deep awareness of yourself and your surrounds, helping you disconnect from racing thoughts and negativity. This is an immersive experience, where a small number of guests are hosted on the temple grounds for a duration of five days or more.

対馬聖山寺

1453 Izuhara-machi, Kokubu,
Tsushima Island, Nagasaki

seizanji.com

Hakata Port to Izuhara Port,
then walk (5min)

TSUSHIMA SEIZANJI TEMPLE
TSUSHIMA ISLAND

Girded by the waters of the strait of Tsushima (and reached by high-speed jet foil or ferry from Hakata), Tsushima Island is mountainous and lush, laying claim to memorable nature walks and the famous leopard cats, whose beautiful, thick spotted fur and lithe physique set them apart from domestic cats. Tsushima Seizanji is a temple stay far away from the crowds and noise, with an emphasis on rest and tranquillity.

Established in the mid to late 800s, the temple has the benefit of both ocean and mountain views (with the added bonus of a city view of Izuhara). You can visit for the day and partake in the zazen (meditation) and Sutra experiences, which provide morning prayers, porridge and pickles, or tea and sweets, enjoyed from the beautiful temple building and grounds.

We love to sleep on futon and tatami in a classic Japanese room and imagine ourselves living the life of the monks centuries ago. However, if you prefer a Western bed and TV, they are available. There are public spaces to relax and unwind and if you need to study or work, there is free wi-fi. Walk the wooden corridors and observe the light and shadow play on the shoji screens. Steep in the communal bath before eating a fortifying dinner. Awake at dawn and watch the sun rise over the mountains. The grounds and surrounding area are perfect for both hiking and cycling and the island location gives Tsushima Seizanji a feeling of true dislocation from your everyday cares.

心を満たす庭園

Mindful
gardens

MINDFUL TIP

The suffix 'en' means 'garden'.

Built by emperors, monks and samurai, Japanese gardens have been revered by all classes of people for generations. Japanese garden origins date back to the 7th century CE when travellers were deeply moved by gardens they had seen in China.

Japanese gardens follow the wabi-sabi principle of perfection in imperfection. Your path will be winding, never straight. A leaf flutters to the ground landing on a raked dry garden. The ageing and patina of bark on trees. The mismatched cobbled bridge that spans a winding river. Notable elements recur in Japanese gardens, including water features (lakes, ponds and waterfalls), bridges, stepping stones and small islands. Beautiful, colourful koi (brocaded carp) school in impressive numbers in waterways, drawing gasps from onlookers. Common plantings include cherry and plum blossoms, maples, ginkgo trees, conifers, hydrangeas, wisteria, peonies, waterlilies and ferns, all positioned carefully to enhance their beauty and planted en-masse for the most dramatic effect. The Japanese reflect inspiring elements of the gardens in their everyday life through potted displays out the front of houses, kokedama (moss balls hanging from eaves), mini courtyards in restaurants and seedpods and dried flowers in store displays.

Visiting a Zen garden (*see* p. 153), was one of the key reasons we saved up for our first trip. Nanzenji (*see* p. 26) was our first garden visit; however, since then we have acquired a taste for a diverse array of garden styles, most notably the Samurai strolling gardens we can visit to unwind in big cities. Set up for strolling by the ruling elite and for the pleasure of feudal lords and samurai, the gardens have since been claimed by the people. Many of our favourite gardens feature traditional teahouses, where we relax with matcha and wagashi (Japanese sweets), whilst looking at the seasonal beauty of the trees and flowers. Take a picnic lunch, make sure you don't have a time limit, sit, stroll, contemplate and just be. Whilst most of our listings are easily accessed city gardens, we have included a few of our favourites worth travelling for.

Whilst in lockdown through COVID, we were inspired to get our local landscape architect Michael to build us our own tiny Japanese garden so that we could relive some of our favourite memories over a cup of green tea.

Previous and opposite top left:
Ritsurin Garden; opposite top
right: Tea and sweets at Rikugien
Garden; opposite bottom: The
Adachi Museum of Art Garden

兼六園

1 Kenrokumachi,
Kanazawa, Ishikawa

pref.ishikawa.jp/siro-niwa/
kenrokuen

Kanazawa station bus to
Kanazawa Castle Park

KENROKUEN GARDEN
KANAZAWA

Strolling through Kenrukoen it is easy to see why it is considered one of the most beautiful gardens in Japan and one of the essential three traditional Japanese landscape gardens. Founded in the Edo period (1603 to 1867) by Kaga's feudal lords, Kenrokuen garden was set up initially as a private strolling garden and was designed to have beauty unveiling as you turned each corner. The name means 'garden with six attributes', employing the traits of the perfect garden: spaciousness, seclusion, artifice, antiquity, waterways and panoramas. The landscape also represents aspects of literature, has allusions to the Noh chant and replicates known features from other landmarks.

The garden has an impressive series of ponds connected by winding waterways. Small groves, fairytale cottages and sculptures dot the undergrowth. In spring, the sakura (cherry blossoms) create pink canopies over bridges and ponds and glow a glorious dark pink when lit up at night. We first visited in autumn when maples leaves floated to the ground, turning the park into a sea of yellow and gold. We returned at dusk when the Yugao-tei teahouse (1774) by the lake was infused with warm yellow light.

A unique feature of the park are the yukitsuri, upside-down cone-like rope structures which support the trees against damage from heavy snow. The garden also contains historic treasures including the oldest fountain in Japan, the Kotoji toro two-legged stone lantern, the 'Flying Geese' bridge and the Kaiseki stone pagoda. A truly remarkable space and one that you'll return to again and again in the garden of your mind.

醍醐寺

DAIGOJI TEMPLE GARDEN
KYOTO

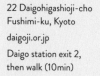

22 Daigohigashioji-cho
Fushimi-ku, Kyoto
daigoji.or.jp
Daigo station exit 2,
then walk (10min)

This Buddhist Shingon Sect temple compound, a UNESCO World Heritage Site that spreads out over the side of a mountain in south-eastern Kyoto, offers a wealth of discovery for the ardent stroller. Lushly planted groves shine in all seasons. Many buildings hold great historical significance, like the Sanbo-in, which once housed the head priest. The compound is also known for Hideyoshi's extravagant cherry blossom viewing party in 1598 CE (what happened at the party stays at the party).

We love Sanboin's wonderful dry garden and small lake, perfect for a mini stroll. The five-tiered pagoda in the Shima Daigo area is Kyoto's oldest building (dating back to 951 CE). The gnarled branches of spectacular weeping cherry trees can be found in various places around the garden, notably around the Reihokan Museum (head there in early April).

Though the compound's history of cherry blossoms is significant, Daigoji makes no apologies about being an autumn garden. Framed vistas of the faded gold, blazing reds and yellows of autumn leaves are a singular pleasure. Daigoji temple boasts a stunning view, a lake spanned by a vermilion bridge which leads towards resplendent Bentendo hall, all ringed by the most glorious autumn trees. Fiery in autumn, the lake, bridge and hall combination provides one of Kyoto's prime photo opportunities.

偕楽園

KAIRAKUEN GARDEN
MITO

1-3-3 Tokiwa-cho
Mito, Ibaraki
ibaraki-kairakuen.jp/access
Direct bus from Mito
station to Kairaku-en bus stop
(or walk 30min along the banks
of Senba lake)

Kairakuen is another of the three best Japanese landscape gardens in Japan, distinguished by its yin-yang garden design philosophy and its plum trees. Built in 1841 by feudal lord Tokugawa Nariaki, Kairakuen was open to members of the working class from its inception, a marked difference to the other two great landscape gardens who were at the time only strollable by the ruling elite.

Sakura (cherry blossom) might be the most famous bloom in Japan, but plum blossoms have an allure of their own and Kairakuen is a spectacular example of how mass planting (there are an estimated 3000 plum trees in 100 different varieties) can produce a truly stunning effect. The time to visit is in late February and throughout March, where you'll not only get to enjoy the beauty of the classic white plum blossom but pink and red blushes as well.

We love the spectacular shakkei (borrowed scenery) views of Lake Senba, best viewed from the top floor of the Kobuntei, a traditional three-storey pavilion. The garden also features an atmospheric bamboo grove, clusters of towering cedars and the historic spring fountain To-gyoku-sen that still bubbles with the precious water once used in the tea ceremony at the Karoan teahouse.

足立美術館

THE ADACHI MUSEUM OF ART GARDEN

YASUGI

320 Furukawacho, Yasugi, Shimane

www.adachi-museum.or.jp

Yasugi station, then shuttle bus

Yasugi and the surrounding Shimane prefecture offer a wealth of unforgettable experiences off the regular tourist trail. A highlight is the Adachi Museum whose garden holds the prestigious title of being named 'Best Garden in Japan' for the past 18 years running.

The museum was the lifelong dream of Zenko Adachi, a local businessman, art collector and passionate gardener. It opened in 1970 when he was in his 71st year. He employed the very best to realise his dream of combining the beauty of both Japanese modern art and gardens into one inspiring complex. Superstar contemporary landscape architect Kinsaku Nakane was entrusted to design the garden and Adachi clearly had an eye for style.

The museum houses a collection of modern and contemporary paintings, the prized pieces in the collection being Yokoyama Taikan's work whom Adachi felt had an affinity with nature. While you can't walk around and explore this wonderful garden, you can view it from various windows, platforms and outdoor spaces within the museum complex. In this sense, the garden itself becomes an exhibit and takes on the form of a living canvas with various spectacular vistas unveiling themselves as you move through the building and its various walkways.

This vast oasis is broken down into five green spaces over 165,000 square metres (40 acres). We contemplated the moss garden, dry garden, pond, white gravel pine and waterfall gardens. We moved around the space transfixed by winding white paths, large rocks and the deep greens, vibrant against the bright blues of the summer sky. The mountainous country backdrop make the perfectly realised spaces seem almost otherworldly.

For a front row garden seat slide into a booth in cafe Midori, drinking coffee while transfixed by spectacular views. On our next visit, we'll take tea at Juraku-an teahouse, and watch the garden from the two long windows viewed as 'living scrolls'.

横浜 三溪園

SANKEIEN GARDEN
YOKOHAMA

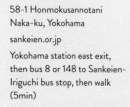

58-1 Honmokusannotani
Naka-ku, Yokohama

sankeien.or.jp

Yokohama station east exit,
then bus 8 or 148 to Sankeien-
Iriguchi bus stop, then walk
(5min)

Built by silk trader Hara Sankei in the late 1800s and early 1900s, Sankeien is one
of Japan's most impressive strolling gardens and testament to Yokohama's power
as a trading port. The vast space, stretching along the coast, is known for cherry
blossom viewing and verdant natural trails that take you out of city life and imbue
you with a feeling that you are walking in country Japan or in Kyoto's hallowed,
sacred groves.

A secret that Sankei wanted to keep to himself, only the outer gardens were
originally open to the public, but the whole garden became accessible in 1953.
Various spectacular blooms and blossoms can be viewed with the changing of the
seasons, including cherry blossoms and yellow roses in spring, waterlilies and lotus
in summer, bush clover in autumn and plum and daffodils in winter.

The grounds feature several buildings of note, 'imported' from various places
around Japan, including the three-tiered pagoda from Tomyoji Temple in Kyoto
(which rises majestically above the trees), an impressive main hall (also from
Tokyoji) and Tokeiji's Buddhist Hall, considered the oldest wooden structure in
Kanto (dating to 1457 CE). Some of our favourite buildings include beautiful
teahouses Kinmokutsu and Choshukaku and a remodelled version of Sankei's
family mansion Kakushokaku. The gashho-style farmhouse of the Yanohara family
is also one of the garden's standout treasures, but much more can be unveiled by
strolling the grounds without any particular aim or direction – it's one of Sankeien
garden's particular joys.

小石川後楽園

KOISHIKAWA KORAKUEN GARDEN
TOKYO

1-6-6 Koraku, Bunkyo, Tokyo

www.tokyo-park.or.jp/teien/en/
koishikawa

Suidobashi station west exit,
then walk (5min)

Being mindful in a frenetic city like Tokyo is not always easy. Koishikawa Korakuen is a haven within the very city centre, one that takes you so far out of the concrete jungle that you'll swear that you have travelled for many hours and discovered a hidden country escape. A gem from the Edo period (1603 to 1867), and one of the three remaining 'daimyo' feudal lord gardens, Koishikawa Korakuen is a perfect patch of green adjacent to the looming bubble of Tokyo Dome City.

As with other landscape gardens, the garden re-creates notable Chinese and Japanese scenery, shaping natural and man-made materials to achieve the desired views that can then be seen from various vantage points around the walking trails. The popular stone 'full moon' bridge, which arches over the lake forming a circular moon shape with the reflection of the water, was designed under the advice of Confucian scholar Shu Shunsui. Tsutenkyo Bridge, a wooden bridge of bright vermilion is also a standout sight and a perfect photo opportunity.

The mass planting of autumn trees makes the garden particularly alluring in late November and early December, although the sakura (cherry blossoms) in late March are obviously also a major drawcard. The close proximity to the northern entrance of the Imperial Palace gardens also makes Koishikawa Korakuen the perfect destination for a day of immersive garden ambling. Like its Okayama namesake, this garden is for 'enjoying later' (korakuen), so maybe indulge in some strenuous shopping beforehand.

六義園

6-16-3 Honko Magome,
Bunkyo, Tokyo

www.tokyo-park.or.jp/teien/en/
rikugien

Komagome station south exit,
then walk (7min)

RIKUGIEN GARDEN
TOKYO

Rikugien garden is a leading landscape garden of the Edo period (1603 to 1867), a transportive haven of green set in easily accessible Bunkyo ward, Tokyo. A true manifestation of the phrase 'small but perfectly formed', Rikugien is walkable within an hour. It's spread out around a beautiful lake with a central island and makes for a wondrous spot to view brightly coloured maple leaves in autumn or the blushing pink of sakura (cherry blossoms) in spring, both which are lit up for a spectacular effect at night. Fat koi float in the waterways and wild birds fly overhead or nest in the trees, making you feel far from the madding crowd. The garden becomes many a Tokyoite's favourite destination in late March when the cherry trees blush pink.

Rikugien garden was overseen by Yanagisawa Yoshiyasu, the 5th Tokugawa shogun's associate, and completed in 1702 CE. The name translates as 'Garden of the Six Principles' – referring to the six elements in traditional Chinese-influenced Waka poetry. There were 88 different parts of the garden which were created based on lines from famous Waka poems and each had a stone marker (now only 32 markers remain). The garden was opened to the public in 1938 by then owner, Mitsubishi founder Iwasaki Yataro, who restored the garden to its former glory after purchasing it in 1878.

Michelle and her friend Hiki planned a visit in deep autumn. Hiki's mother dressed Michelle in an autumn-coloured kimono, a family heirloom. Hiki's kimono was emblazoned with blue butterflies. They started their day by taking tea and wagashi (Japanese sweets) at the Meiji-period (1868 to 1912) Fukiage tearoom. Then, analogue cameras in hand, took close-up shots of the garden's foliage, and images of each other in the autumnal garden and on the many bridges spanning the lakes and flowing streams.

後楽園

KORAKUEN GARDEN
OKAYAMA

Originally built in 1700, and modernised in 1863, Korakuen is one of the three most revered strolling gardens in Japan, along with Kenrokuen garden (*see* p. 156) and Kairakuen garden (*see* p. 159). This beautiful landscaped garden has many delightful vistas. Vast ponds, streams and winding stone paths tell a story as you move around the garden. Climb Yuishinzan Hill where you can take in views of the whole garden, as well as admire nearby Okayama Castle, an outside treasure that becomes shakkei (borrowed scenery). Standout features include the Samurai house Enyo-tei, a traditional archery range and a crane aviary.

Plantings are plentiful, with particular emphasis on cherry and plum blossom groves. Plums bloom in late February to early March, and cherry viewing is in late March to early April. The weeping cherries by Eisho Bridge are perfect if you are visiting in late April and missed sakura (cherry blossom) season. Other impressive plantings include azaleas, irises, peony and lotus. We were struck by a grid of nine rice paddies situated in the formal garden based on a Confuscian tax philosophy.

In midwinter, after admiring the garden and slipping out the back way to view Okayama Castle (your ticket lets you out and then back in), we stopped for respite in the garden's beautiful Fukuda teahouse. We drank a much-needed hot whisked matcha and ate the teahouse's unique specialty, kibidango (sweet millet dumplings) whilst admiring the picturesque garden scene through the teahouse's large round viewing window.

1-5 Korakuen
Kita-ku, Okayama
okayama-korakuen.jp
Direct Bus from
Okayama station

栗林公園

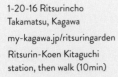

1-20-16 Ritsurincho
Takamatsu, Kagawa

my-kagawa.jp/ritsuringarden

Ritsurin-Koen Kitaguchi
station, then walk (10min)

RITSURIN GARDEN
TAKAMATSU

If you are planning to visit the art islands of Naoshima and Teshima, why not do as we did and take the ferry, stay the night in Takamatsu and wake up with an early morning garden stroll in Ritsurin garden? Often considered the fourth of the three great Japanese landscape gardens, Ritsurin garden has a history that impressively stretches back to 1642 CE. Opened to the public in 1875, it's one of Japan's best examples of a preserved Edo-period (1603 to 1867) garden, and it exhibits many of the traits that made that period's gardens so treasured by the Japanese people.

Constructed with strolling in mind, the garden is specifically arranged in a series of views discovered as you move around the garden. Michelle's second visit was with two girlfriends early one Takamatsu morning. They wandered the garden as if it was their own private backyard. A gentle English-speaking park volunteer took time to explain the garden's history and escorted them to Hiraiho Hill which, he explained, was made in the image of Mount Fuji and was the best view in the park.

The panorama spread out before the open tatami-mat room of the Kikugetsutei teahouse is inspiring. Kimono-clad hosts serve tea while you observe breathtaking views of the garden from all four sides, including the charming Engetsukyo, 'Crescent Moon' Bridge, which arches over South Pond.

Sensitive to the seasons, Ritsurin garden is particularly popular in spring for the cherry blossoms (which are illuminated at night) and also for resplendent autumn colours. The pine trees are the park's darlings, especially the 'three great pines': Hakomatsu (box pine), Niagara Goyomatsu (a rare Japanese white pine that has grown from a bonsai) and the Tsurukamematsu (crane and turtle pine). If you're feeling adventurous, take a tour of the garden from a lake's eye view in one of the Wasen boats.

由志園

YUUSHIEN GARDEN
DAIKONSHIMA ISLAND

1260-2 Yatsuka-cho Hanyu,
Shimane

yuushien.com

Bus 70-1, 70-2 or 70-3 from
Matsue station across causeway
to island

Daikonshima (Radish Island) resides in the middle of Lake Nakaumi in Matsue, and is home to Yuushien garden, a spectacular haven for floral planting off the tourist radar. For over 300 years, the prefecture of Shimane has been known for its peony flowers and Korean ginseng, both proudly highlighted at Yuushien garden.

The garden takes up a staggering 40,000 square metres (10 acres) of garden spaces, but feels intimate as you move around waterways, weaving in and out of conceptual planting and perfectly manicured trees. Take time to participate in the traditional tea ceremony at Ichibo teahouse while you ponder the story of the eight-headed dragon at Ryuukeidaki waterfall.

Seasonal plantings are meticulously planned to highlight the beauty of the flowers. The peonies bloom all year round in the Peony House. However, if you are lucky enough to visit in late May to early June, the peony festival is a sight to behold. Some 20,000 Japanese peony trees bloom brightly in the daytime and are underlit at dusk. A display of over 3000 flowers float in waterways creating a sea of different shades of pink as far as the eye can see. There are an astounding 250 varieties including rare winter peonies that burst with colour in the colder months.

Bring a picnic lunch or eat at one of the three fine restaurants which serve up food made from fresh local produce, with garden-grown Korean ginseng used to flavour some of the dishes. Plan your own mindful Shimane prefecture retreat visiting the Adachi Museum of Art (see p. 160), staying at Koyokan Ryokan (see p. 120) and making time for a relaxing bath at Matsue Shinjiko Onsen.

心を満たす森林浴

Mindful
forest
bathing

The term shinrin yoku, or forest bathing, was created as recently as 1980 by the Japanese Ministry of Agriculture, Forestry and Fisheries in recognition that many Japanese people needed access to nature to escape the negative impact of spending too much time in the big cities. In the height of summer many Japanese people head to the forest instead of the beach. Like a swim in the ocean or a soak in an onsen (hot spring), bathing in natural forested surrounds relaxes you – helps you absorb positivity and release negativity. Switching off your tech for the day allows for a complete retooling of your attitude. Forest therapy re-establishes a human connection with nature. The vibrations you pick up from giving an ancient tree a good hugging help reduce the production of stress hormones and restore harmony and balance, freeing up rooms in your mind which you can devote to more creative pursuits. The exercise reduces blood pressure and promotes fitness, which helps strengthen the immune system.

If a tree fell in the woods, would anyone hear it? You can ponder this age-old question while immersing yourself deep in nature, inspecting moss, feeling the bark on trees and noticing the light beams hit you sporadically as they try and make their way through the thick canopy of forest leaves.

Japan boasts some of the world's most astounding geography. Rugged, unbridled natural landscapes feature dense forests and waterfalls, making for some of the most memorable trails for the serious hiker or the novice woodland walker. We've trekked through the snow to watch monkeys bathing in hot springs, walked to outdoor onsen in midsummer, and witnessed the unbelievable autumn and spring colour in multiple forest walks.

Japanese forests are primal and ancient, leafy and lush. They appear on mountains or in valleys. They can be nearly impenetrable, or set up with walkable trails that range from breezy to determined. Forests can be in easy reach of cities or far from where you are, a destination promising great rewards. The forest might have notable sights or may be notable in itself, replete with moss or towering cedars. Whether you are escaping for a day or selecting a destination for a trekking holiday, the forest will enrich, embrace and enfold you.

Previous: Minoo Park; *opposite top left:* Sagano Bamboo Forest; *opposite top right:* Yakushima Island; *opposite bottom:* Mount Takao

苔の森

Yakōri, Sakuho,
Minamisaku-gun, Nagano

Chino station, then bus (1hr)

KOKENOMORI (MOSS FOREST)
SAKUHO

The forest around peaceful Shirakoma Pond sits in Nagano prefecture's
Eastern Mountain range, in the lush glades reclining between Mount Aka and
Mount Morai. The area's climate sees regular rainfall which, in turn, over centuries
has given rise to a dreamy moss forest. The light falls differently here, filtering
through the trees, illuminating the luxurious carpet of green which sparkles with
tiny diamonds of dew. The forest trail around the pond takes around 35 minutes.
A garland of springy moss dresses the twisted roots of trees, blessing you with
nature's natural tones and textures, an enchanting colour palette of deep greens
smothering rusty browns. In autumn, the leaves of the trees are a radiant red,
contrasting with the green, a stunning sight reflected in the mirror-like stillness
of Shirakoma Pond.

There are over 480 species of moss in the forest, each having its own shape,
texture and personality. Ten spots are marked along the trail, highlighting
different mossy environments. Tread softly and notice each step. Mori (forest)
and Mosu (moss) girls gather, magnifying glass in hand, inspecting flecks and
fronds. Michelle became fascinated by Mori and Mosu girls over 10 years ago
(she has her own vintage magnifying glass). They came to her attention through
a Japanese fashion magazine, which showed girls in long dresses made from linens
and other natural fibres, inquisitively inspecting lichen and moss in magical forest
scapes. To them, the forest is a spiritual glade.

Make sure to visit Takamiishi-Koya lodge along the trail for a spectacular view of
the lake. Be sure to stay on the trails and wooden pathways provided so as not to
disturb the delicate biosphere. From mid-November to mid-April the road to the
forest is closed because of the winter snow.

嵐山竹林

Arashiyama, Ukyo-ku

Randen-Saga station,
then walk (10min)

SAGANO BAMBOO GROVE
ARASHIYAMA

Arashiyama or 'Storm Mountain' makes an immediate impression on you as soon as you arrive. The township is misplaced in time, with old-world shops and eateries set against a backdrop of misty mountains and the Togetsukyo (moon crossing) bridge which stretches lazily over the Katsura river. Small temples and shrines dot the area, including Tenryuji, Koggenji and Shakakuji, which circle the famous Sagano Bamboo Grove.

The 500-metre-long (1640-foot) glade is a natural cluster of moso (turtle shell) bamboo, developed in the Heian period (794 to 1185 CE) and perfected in the 1930s. The towering green spires of bamboo form cathedral-like arches. The lofty, thin reeds bend slightly in the wind, shifting the filtered light, stalks groaning ever so slightly and occasionally colliding with a melancholy 'plock'. The musical sound made the list of '100 Soundscapes of Japan'.

There is something intrinsically Japanese about bamboo – handcrafts, the shakuhachi (bamboo flutes), bridges, scaffolding, roofs and the flavour of crisp bamboo shoots – it's used in so many ways to enhance everyday life in Japan that it's become a symbol. To see it growing in its natural habitat imbues it with a mesmerising intensity. It's a notably different kind of forest bathing. We recommend an early morning or dusk visit to avoid crowds and witness the gentle sounds of the holy sanctuary, broken now and then by the chirrup of a fossicking bird. The quiet stills the soul and the reverence for the versatile, eco-friendly plant excites the mind.

箇面公園

MINOO PARK
OSAKA

A sidestep from Osaka's crowded hub, Minoo Park offers a welcome respite. Perfect for hiking and nature walks, the Meiji-period (1868 to 1912) park was included in '100 Best Forest Bathing locations' (1986). It takes around an hour to complete and the 3km walk alongside a stream and is paved, which is a gift for strollers who don't fare well on uneven ground.

Minoo's highlights emerge suddenly from the undergrowth as you walk along, culminating in a picture-perfect snap of a vermilion stone-arch bridge languishing in front of the gently cascading Minoo waterfall. The 300-metre (984-foot) waterfall gives its name to the park. A minoo is a 'winnow basket' that separates grains from husks – a shape formed in the rock-face. Aesthetic monks have used the waterfall for meditation as far back as the 7th century. There are nearly 1000 different types of plants in the park, including century-old trees and Japanese maples. If you visit at the end of November, there's a canopy of red autumn leaves that forms an exquisite vista, layering the bridge, trees and falls in an impressive three-dimensional tableau.

Narrow roads in the park are flanked by tiny food stalls, souvenir and craft shops – in autumn try the local seasonal snack, momiji (maple leaf) tempura. Peaceful Shotengu Saikoji temple leads to a beautiful walk along the Takamichi trail. The park's Ryuanji temple (658 CE) is the birthplace of the lottery and luck, blessings and good fortune are your spiritual rewards.

1-18 Minookoen, Minoo, Osaka

mino-park.jp

Minoo station, then walk (5min)

屋久島

Yakushima Tourist Association
799 Miyanoura, Yakushima,
Kumage district, Kagoshima

yesyakushima.com

Jetfoil from Kagoshima Port
to Yakushima Miyanoura or
Anbo Port

YAKUSHIMA ISLAND
KAGOSHIMA

Reached by hydrofoil from Kagoshima's ferry terminal, Yakushima is one of the world's great secrets – a UNESCO World Heritage–listed island where the towering cypress trees and alien granite of the mountaintops are the island's skyscrapers. The wet climate here makes for a magical paradise of moss. Forest bathing in Yakushima draws on a deeper magic. No wonder it was the setting for Studio Ghibli's *Princess Mononoke*.

The forests are populated by ancient cedars, ranging from a mind-boggling 1000 to 7000 years old. Known as Yasugi, a contraction of Yakushima Sugi (cedar), the trees lord over the forest, ancient beings shrouded in green moss cloaks with tortured root systems winding around rocks and stone steps. The rain is relentless (locals joke that 'it rains 35 days a month') and this makes the forest permanently lush. Raging waterfalls, dew-kissed branches, sunlight struggling through the tangled trees – this is the stuff of mythology.

Several trails wind through the forest undergrowth. The Arakawa and Shiratani Unsuikyo trails are a spiritual pilgrimage toward 7000-year-old Jomon Sugi, the ancient cedar, oldest and wisest tree on the island (Shiratani also passes the 3000-year-old Yayoi Sugi). Mountain lovers will want to tackle the Yodogawa trail which leads to Yakushima's tallest peak, Mount Miyanoura. The Onoaida trail begins and ends at charming Onoaida Onsen taking in delightful Senpiro-no-taki Falls along the way.

Travel around the island is by bus. Make sure to take enough yen with you, as ATMs and credit card facilities are rare.

高尾山

Keio Takaosanguchi station
building, 2241, Takaomachi,
Hachioji

tokyotouristinfo.com/en/detail/
M0021

Takaosanguchi station, then
chairlift, cable car or walk

MOUNT TAKAO
HACHIOJI

Mount Takao has forest bathing, excellent hiking and a sacred temple, all
reachable as a daytrip from Tokyo. The first thing you'll notice is the station, a
startling modernist makeover by architect Kengo Kuma, who formed a curved
structure from the area's spectacular cedarwood, mimicking the mountain's
temple, Yakuoin. Unusually, the station is home to contemporary Onsen Keio
Takaosan, so do like we do and reserve time to relax.

Catch the funicular railway or pop-coloured retro chairlift up the mountain.
The vistas of the mountain greenery and Tokyo's distant metropolitan sprawl,
particularly on the way down, are breathtaking.

Walking is the main pastime on Mount Takao and it's a virtual choose-your-own-
adventure of trails. The creatively named hike number 1 is the most popular and
accessible path, but following one of the lesser-trodden pathways will give you a
calmer and more secluded walking experience. Torii gates, statues, giant cedars
and impressive viewpoints (including iconic Mount Fuji), dot the mountaintop.
The 'Octopus Tree' has a prodigious root system resembling tentacles. If you
missed the sakura (cherry blossoms) season in Tokyo, you'll be happy to know
that they arrive fashionably late to the party at Mount Takao.

Takao-san Yakuoin is Japan's third-oldest Buddhist temple (founded in 744 CE)
and home to a group of aesthetic monks, the Shugendo, who meditate
under nearby waterfalls and walk on fire (you can actually join them in both
of these practices without prior arrangement). The stunning Nio-Mon gate
leads to extensive and forested temple grounds, perfect for a spot of spiritual
forest bathing.

心を満たす巡礼路

Mindful
pilgrimage
trails

For travellers wishing to find a more spiritual connection to Japan, a pilgrimage trail combines nature, philosophy, religion and often strenuous hiking. Japan's pilgrimage trails are among the best treks in the world. You will encounter a staggering range of impressive and ancient temples, religious statues and talisman, roadside ryokan (traditional Japanese inns), shukubo (pilgrim and temple lodgings) onsen and shops owned by generations of makers and crafters.

Pilgrimage trails aren't just for pilgrims, though. You don't have to be on a spiritual quest to enjoy the sights and scenery. You don't have to be lost to find yourself. The deep silence of the forest and the age and significance of your encounters will give you an enlightenment of sorts and instil in you a deep sense of peace and gratitude. Have your own reasons and make your own discoveries.

You can tackle a pilgrimage in stages, selecting sections of track or specific monuments and temples as you go. Some people book a holiday specifically so they can experience a whole trail, taking time out from work to have a life-altering experience, to see their lives through a new lens or to meditate on a recent life-changing event.

Consider your own fitness and pick the trail you can handle. Also consider your equipment carefully, as this is rugged and sometimes dangerous terrain at the mercy of all kinds of weather conditions. You'll need sturdy boots and a backpack with essentials, some food and why not a journal so, like the poet Basho, you can observe along the way, make comments, record memories and compose verse. Prepare to be moved, entranced, altered and to emerge a better and, yes, a fitter, you.

Previous: Pilgrimage hats and bags in Matsuyama (88 Temple Pilgrimage); *opposite:* Images from along Nakasendo Way

中山道

NAKASENDO WAY
KANSAI, CHUBU AND KANTO REGIONS

Starting at Old Edo (Tokyo)
and ending at Kyoto

nakasendoway.com

Originally established for samurai, shogun and feudal lords to travel, in order for the Tokugawa shogunate to maintain order between the two major cities, the Nakasendo (central mountain) Way is a postal route shaped in the 8th century and once linked Old Edo (Tokyo) to Kyoto. It stretches for an estimated 534 kilometres (332 miles) and takes in some stunning locations in Saitama, Gunma, Nagano, Gifu and Shiga. The route featured 69 stations, or rest stops, immortalised in a series of Ukiyo-e prints by Utagawa Hiroshige and Keisai Eisen. It is no longer intact, with stretches of the road claimed by highways, paved roads and paths. However, several parts of the trail remain in their original form, most notably the trail through the Kiso Valley leading toward Magome-juku (preserved postal town), the 43rd of the 69 stations. Many minshuku (family-run bed and breakfasts) dot the way and are recommended for authentic overnight stays and making connections with locals.

We walked the trail between Magome-juku and Tsumago-juku which featured beautiful original dark wood buildings (they hide any signs of contemporary life here to preserve the experience), huddled together and leaning ever so slightly this way or that to form a crooked nursery rhyme vista. Longstanding makers plied their trade in centuries-old souvenir craft stalls. Around each corner of this part of the trail was a magical scene: streams with waterwheels, gnarled trees and stone lanterns all with a glorious mountain backdrop. The seasoned hiker can turn this into a multi-day trek with a bit of forward planning and the canny use of the occasional train connection. Picturesque villages Nojiri and Narai connect stunning vistas, bamboo groves, cobbled walkways, waterfalls and forests of cedar. Karuizawa to Yokokawa takes you over the Usui-toge pass, which affords memorable mountain views.

A historical pilgrimage rather than a spiritual one, the Nakasendo Way offers the mindful traveller a chance to hop into a time machine and explore nature and life as it was in slower and gentler times.

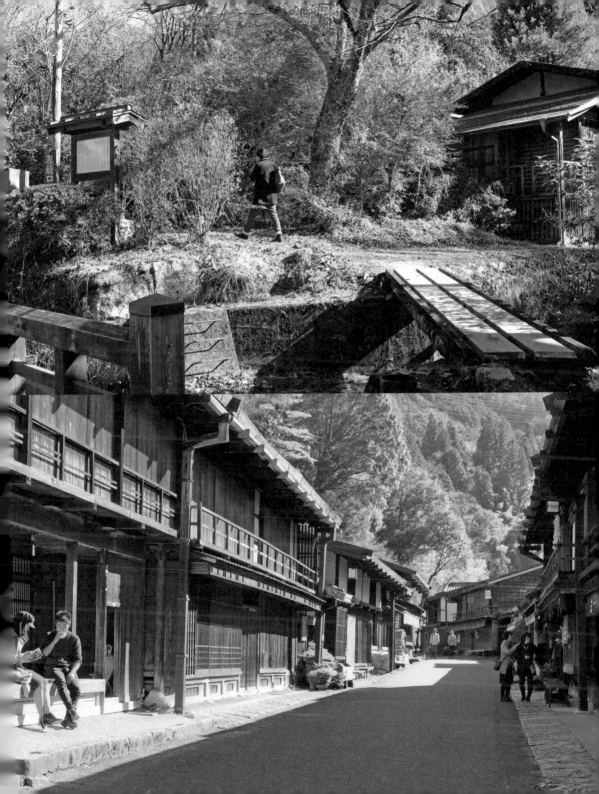

西国三十三所

SAIGOKU KANNON PILGRIMAGE
KANSAI REGION

Starting at Seigantoji,
Wakayama, and ending
at Kegonji, Gifu
jh-saikoku33.jp/en

The Saigoku Kannon Pilgrimage dates back 1300 years and is regarded as the first pilgrim route in Japan. It takes in 33 Buddhist temples, centred in Kyoto but expanding outward to the Kansai region. It focuses on the Kannon, or Bodhisattva of compassion, enshrined in each temple. If you pray at each site, and devote your life to others, you can be reborn into paradise.

The 33 Kannon can be found in Kyoto, Shiga, Gifu, Nara, Wakayama, Osaka and Hyogo. Like many hikers, adopt the traditional pilgrim attire and walking stick. Begin at Seigantoji in Wakayama. Temple number two, Kimiidera, is known as the first temple to bloom in sakura (cherry blossom) season. Kokawadera, the largest temple compound on the route, dates to an impressive 770 CE and features a pre-Edo period dry garden.

Without doubt, the most famous temple on the route is Kyoto's breathtaking Kiyomizudera, established in 978 CE, a UNESCO World Heritage–listed site. Set high on wooden stilts, the striking dark wood temple with the thick thatched roof is offset by vibrant greens in summer and burnished golds in autumn, one of Japan's most photographed vistas. The final temple of the pilgrimage is Kegon-ji in Gifu.

Overall, it's possible to visit all of the temples by bus and train or hire car, walking some of the way. The pilgrimage is around 1000 kilometres (621 miles) which of course takes time and dedication, perfect for pilgrims but not so great for anyone on a limited holiday. Most people visit the temples separately and in various life stages.

MINDFUL TIP

Famous temples along the way included Rokkakudo in Kyoto, the birthplace of ikebana (*see* p. 84) and Shohoji in Shiga, where Basho composed his most enduring haiku:

the old pond,
a frog jumps in
the sound of water

熊野古道

KUMANO KODO PILGRIMAGE
KII PENINSULA

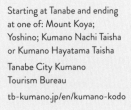

Starting at Tanabe and ending
at one of: Mount Koya;
Yoshino; Kumano Nachi Taisha
or Kumano Hayatama Taisha

Tanabe City Kumano
Tourism Bureau

tb-kumano.jp/en/kumano-kodo

Kumano Kodo is an ancient pilgrimage trail that leads inland from (and at some points around) the coast of the Kii Peninsula in southern Kansai. Designated a UNESCO World Heritage Site in 2004, the route links three shrines: Hongu, Hayatama and Nachi Taishas, collectively known as the Kumano Sanzan. The trek itself acts as a devotional path, with pilgrims proving themselves by traversing treacherous and perilous terrain.

Over the years four main trails have been established. The most walked is the Nakahechi Imperial route, which begins at Tanabe on the west coast and links the three shrines. It's perfect for a hiking itinerary that spans several days and the terrain is the easiest to tackle. Aside from the shrines, you'll encounter small villages providing local accommodation; the delightfully rustic Toganoki-jaya teahouse; and Takahara, the 'village in the mist'.

On the Ohechi Coastal route you will occasionally emerge from the undergrowth to find yourself staring at an expansive view of the Pacific Ocean. The Iseji Eastern route also has beach views, as well as tiered rice fields, orchards, tea fields and bamboo groves. The mountainous Kohechi route cuts a north-to-south swathe through the centre of the peninsula and links the Kumano Sanzan to Mount Koya. Along the way you'll encounter the Hatenashi settlement, called the 'Village in the Sky', 400 metres (1312 feet) above sea level, a village of great beauty with stunning views.

出羽三山

DEWA SANZAN PILGRIMAGE
TSURUOKA

Tsuruoka, Yamagata

dewasanzan.com

Yamagata station to
Tsuruoka station, then
bus to Mount Haguro

A combined pilgrimage, forest bathe and energetic hike, the Dewa Sanzan
are three mountains that hold great spiritual importance in Japan. Situated
in northern Honshu's Yamagata prefecture, east of the Sea of Japan's Shonai
coast, pilgrims have been coming here for spiritual revival and personal
renaissance for over 1400 years. Each of the three moutains: Haguro, Gassan
and Yudono, have a memorable and important shrine at or near their peak. The
Yamabushi (mountain worshipping) monks, clad in their checked robes and
carrying picturesque paper lanterns, ascend the peaks during Aki-no-mini-iri
(Autumn Peak Ritual), and Fuyu-no-mini-iri (Winter Peak Ritual).

Begin by climbing Mount Haguro, which is 414 metres (1358 feet) and is open all
year round. Its denoted 'cosmic time' is the present, and its gift is strength to deal
with the world's current adversities. The mountain features colossal ancient cedars
including one, dubbed the 'Grandfather Cedar', which is 43 metres (141 feet)
tall and an estimated 1000 years old. Climb the cobbled path to the five-tiered
pagoda, a towering, ornate wooden structure circa 931 CE. Draped in snow, it
is one of the most enthralling things you'll ever see. Your ultimate destination is
Sanjin-Gosaiden, a shrine which boasts the thickest thatch roof in Japan.

Mount Gassan is 1940 metres (6365 feet) and open from July to mid-October
for hiking and April to July for skiing. Its 'cosmic time' is the past and Mount
Gassan is placed at the border of the afterlife. Its gift is peace with your ancestors.
Your goal is the Mount Gassan Shrine where, on a clear day, you can see all the
way to the Sea of Japan.

The third mountain, Mount Yudono, stands at a height of 1503 metres
(4931 feet). Its 'cosmic time' is the future, and its gift is facing your future self.
The Mount Yudono Shrine is your objective, but note that it is only open during
Golden Week (late April/early May).

Pilgrims can don ceremonial robes to make the journey into the mountains.
Be mindful of each step along the way, stop and observe small details and store
memories and experiences.

四国遍路

SHIKOKU HENRO (88 TEMPLE PILGRIMAGE)

SHIKOKU

Starting at Ryozenji in
Tokushima and ending at
Okuboji in Kagawa

shikoku-tourism.com/en/
shikoku-henro

The island of Shikoku is best known for the Shikoku Henro, or 88 Temple
Pilgrimage, a trail around the circumference of the island. Dating back to the
16th century, with a possible inception several centuries earlier, the trail is around
1200 kilometres (745 miles) long and takes 30 to 60 days. Many Japanese
people make the pilgrimage to memorialise loved ones, to pray for their family's
wellbeing or for their own spiritual nurture.

Walking the entire way is a philosophical and physical endurance test with many
rewards. Temples along the way are truly memorable and connecting with locals,
sleeping in and around shukubo (temple lodgings), or staying at minshuku (bed
and breakfasts) forms lasting memories. The walk is said to have the potential
to change your life, or at least change the person you are.

To make your trek more authentic, wear the ceremonial white hakui (cotton
overcoat) of the Ohenro, and the sugegasa (conical hat). You will also need a
kongozue (traditional walking stick) and a Sutra book, a monk's bag and a bell.
Most people complete the route in a clockwise direction beginning with temple
number one – Ryozenji in Tokushima.

Start at Naruto and walk west along the Yoshino river where you'll find the first
11 temples in close proximity. Ryozenji's stunning wooden gate sets the scene.
Temple five, Jizoji, has 200 statues, each with different facial expressions. Temple
eight, Kumadaniji, features what is considered to be the oldest gate on the
entire trail (it dates to 1687). Along the way, towering pagodas rise above dense
mountain foliage, buildings show the patina of hundreds of years and lichen and
moss-flecked stone Buddha statues watch benignly over twisting cobbled paths.

Mid-March to May and also October and November are the recommended
times to make the trek. Select a section of the trail and take your time – or you
can utilise the chartered bus, cycle or hire a car.

Mindful
attractions

Dear Readers,

In this special chapter, we'd like to introduce you to a small collection of our favourite mindful locations, adventures and pastimes that have stayed with us and created forever memories. They are places that give us pause, are uniquely Japanese, but with a universal beauty and reverence. When travelling we make a pact to notice things that we wouldn't normally notice. We collect our thoughts and discuss observations over tea and wagashi (Japanese sweets), or over a sake and dinner.

Exceptional mindful experiences can be found in major cities, country towns or deep in tangled forests. Knee-deep in vibrant flowers, lost in nature; touching history in revered and silent spaces; exploring the way of life and prodigious output of artisans, archivists and creators, are all part of Japan's mindful palette. Small moments can be found in everyday life, local spaces, daily rituals, pockets of calm and moments of stillness. Residential homes displaying potted plants, bonsai and kokedama (moss balls) ensconced within the concrete jungle; details on old buildings; the scent of flowers in the rain; or the subtle, intricate movements of ceremonies and observances. Then there are the big, unmissable things, ancient monuments, towering modern structures and arresting nature.

Whilst we have a chapter on Zen, we did not want to leave out the beauty and stillness of the Shinto religion. Shinto floats through the pilgrimage chapter and lives within parks, garden strolls and shinrin yoku (forest bathing). One of our favourite Shinto shrines appears in this chapter (but once you know what they look like, you will see them everywhere). You will encounter stunning mountain temples, ancient shrines, craftspeople's homes, poet memorials, incomparable cherry blossom views and more – all part of Japan's extraordinary array of experiences.

Steve and Michelle.

Previous and opposite top left:
Nanshoso; *opposite top right*
and bottom: Risshakuji Temple
(Yamadera)

河井寬次郎記念館

569 Gojozaka, Kaneicho,
Higashiyama-ku, Kyoto
Kiyomizu-Gojo station,
then walk (12min)

KAWAI KANJIRO'S HOUSE
KYOTO

Famed early Showa-period (1926 to 1989) folk artist Kawai Kanjiro lived and worked in this house which is now an inspiring museum. One of Japan's best-known potter's homes, this is a must-visit for lovers of slow arts and students of pottery and architecture. Kanjiro's purpose-built machiya (traditional wooden townhouse) has latticed wooden windows, crème plaster walls and dark wood floors matching thick ceiling beams. Tatami-mat rooms have open fireplaces, shoji screens and ornate windows opening onto a tranquil, verdurous garden.

Take off your shoes and put on the slippers provided, this is sacred ground where you'll be taken from concept to completion in a series of rooms which display many of Kanjiro's best works. Rooms are a snapshot of Kanjiro's life, preserved tableaux of the various objects in his abode. His ceramic works are displayed in cases and placed about the house on tables and stands, or as vases (now filled with fresh flowers).

One of the founding members of the mingei (folk craft movement) Kanjiro dedicated his life to pottery, experimenting with glazes and firing techniques. His modest ceramics were inspired by nature and humanity (he refused the offer of 'Living National Treasure' status), keeping to a palette of cobalt, deep reds, coppers and browns. After he died, they shut the doors of his house and later, barely touched, it reopened to the public – a living testament to how the great potter spent his days.

His modernist influences shine through as you stroll through the stunning rooms. Eventually you'll arrive outside to marvel at the impressive eight-chambered noborigama kiln 'Shokei' where Kanjiro fired his creations. His huge climbing kilns populate the exterior of the house. We shut our eyes and imagined the master at work here, slowly going about his creative life.

ファーム富田

15 Go Kisenkita,
Nakafurano, Sorachi

farm-tomita.co.jp

Naka Furano station,
then walk (25min)

FARM TOMITA
FURANO

A 2.5-hour bus trip from Sapporo to Furano will find you striding through brightly coloured fields of lavender. There are several lavender fields to visit, but Farm Tomita is our favourite, a sprawling garden striped with vibrant purple, white, red and green rainbowing out across the fields as far as the eye can see. Tomita presents itself as a country escape where you can envelop yourself in bright fields of flowers. The lavender is the star, smothering the north-east field in swathes of purple (mid-July is prime viewing time) or appearing between exhilarating rows of vibrant poppies, catchfly and baby's breath. Irodori field is where the most photos are understandably snapped – a large canvas of vivid blooms.

However, other fields shine in their own seasons. We love the autumn field whose spider flowers bloom nearly all year-round and create a brightly coloured foreground for the snow-capped Tokachi mountains in winter. The spring field dazzles with bright plantings of Iceland and oriental poppies. The white birch forest in autumn is a crowded square of ghostly trunks crowned in glorious gold. You can visit a greenhouse all year round to see a lavender field. Don't forget to head to Café René to try the lavender soft-serve ice-cream.

Vibrant, glorious and exhilarating, a trip to Farm Tomita lavender fields is a must for any nature lover. And, as you can imagine, it smells like heaven.

ひたち海浜公園

552-18 Ajigaura, Hitachinaka, Ibaraki

hitachikaihin.jp/en

Katsuta station, then bus to Hitachi Seaside Park (15min)

HITACHI SEASIDE PARK

IBARAKI

Once nothing but sand dunes, Hitachi Seaside Park is now reborn as a garden of earthly delights, boasting impressive ocean views. Depending on the season, the park blooms with roses, daffodils, narcissus, poppies, plums and feathery pampas grass.

Among our favourite plantings here are the fields of kochia (summer cypress) which turn an impressive green from mid-July to late September, then a spectacular fiery red and burnished gold in October. From mid-April to early May, walk to the top of Miharashi Hill through the carpet of pastel blue nemophilia (baby blue eyes). The view from the top of the hill is an expansive canvas, the blue of the nemophilia blending with the waters of the Pacific Ocean and the vast skies. Michelle likes to dress in tone, wearing her blue picnic dress and wandering around in the fresh 'country meets the sea' air. Buy some bento boxes at Shinagawa station and a soft-serve ice-cream at the park and lunch amongst nature.

A great way to get your bearings in the enormous park is to jump on and off their adorable mini train. The park also has bike hire (including bicycles for two) and a cycling circuit which takes you through the forested area and along the seaside coast. Attempt the sunflower maze, which leads to a preserved kominka (traditional old house) village, Miharashi no Sato, a recreation of Edo-period (1603 to 1867) farmhouses situated amongst a seasonal flower setting.

There is also a herb garden and an eco-area which prides itself on its conservation. You can get involved in the conservation of the park, or try pottery and craft workshops. Do check the flora calendar before your visit so you are completely informed about what is in season. When at home during COVID Michelle watches the Hitachi video (hitachikaihin.jp/en) to feel part of the changing colours of the seasons.

芭蕉堂

1 Yamanaka Onsen,
Higashi-machi, Kaga

Kaga Onsen Station bus to
Yamanaka Onsen, then walk
(15min)

BASHO-DO HUT

YAMANAKA

'Who needs the dew of youth from the chrysanthemum when
You have the restoring waters of
Yamanaka?'

So said the great haiku poet Basho about one of his three favourite onsen towns.
Basho lived and worked in the mid to late 1600s. A life devoted to poetry, he
wandered far and wide, living each small moment, experiencing life each day at a
time. Basho's poetry talks in short stanzas of nature, yearning, of cities and towns.
A humanist at heart, his quiet genius constructed everyday words into one of
the simplest yet complex forms of poetry, the haiku. Yamanaka was the perfect
inspiration, famous for its onsen water which Basho said 'seeps toward the core
of the body and enriches you both physically and mentally'.

His ode to Yamanaka Onsen over 300 years ago is now commemorated in
a magical hut in a forested area near Kurotani Bridge, where insect buzz and
birdsong compete with the rushing waters of Kakusenkei Gorge. Humble
Basho-do sits in a grove with a small statue of Basho and a plaque featuring
his poem inside. The small hut with light walls, a humble wooden door and large
gabled roof, perched in enchanting nature and eerily lit up in the half-light, is a
magical testament to the famed haiku poet. We visited on Christmas day in the
late afternoon. This was our religious experience, alone in the forest surrounded
by poetry and nature.

Higashiyama Bonheur cafe, secreted in the forest glade, is perched next to
the hut, exuding old-world charm but with an interior of contemporary, minimalist
cool. We ordered our Christmas late afternoon tea of coffee and cake and talked
of the life Basho must have led. It's a place Basho would happily have taken time
out to recharge, and possibly write a poem about the space.

厳島神社

ITSUKUSHIMA SHRINE
MIYAJIMA ISLAND

The island of Miyajima holds one of Japan's oldest shrines, a complex spanning the water and which features Japan's most celebrated torii gate (a symbol of the transition from the mundane to the sacred). At high tide, the gate appears to 'float on the water'. It's one of Japan's most memorable sights and one that transports you to another plane of thought and experience.

Our adventure started when we left the port near Miyajimaguchi station. The leisurely 10-minute ferry trip across the bay eventually rounds the bluff, giving you your first glimpse of Itsukushima's torii gate. We enjoyed the 'sea view' of the gate, meditating upon its age and majesty before arriving on Miyajima Island.

1-1 Miyajimacho, Hatsukaichi, Hiroshima

en.itsukushimajinja.jp

Ferry from port near Miyajimaguchi station

A Heian-period (794 to 1185 CE) Shinto shrine, Itsukushima was built over 900 years ago and has, since 1643, been ranked as one of the 'Three Views of Japan'. The shrine complex, overlooked by sacred Mount Misen, has 19 buildings, in vermilion and white, the majority on stilts, all just above water level when the tide is high. The buildings, including a Noh theatre, are connected by a series of skeletal boardwalks and are spectacular and atmospheric when lit up at night.

司馬遼太郎記念館

SHIBA RYOTARO MEMORIAL MUSEUM LIBRARY

OSAKA

3-11-18 Shimokosaka,
Higashiosaka

shibazaidan.or.jp

Yaenosato station,
then walk (5min)

Ryotaro Shiba (Teiichi Fukuda) was known as a key figure of mid- to late-20th-century literature. His historical novels are widely read and many have been made into popular films. The breath-stealing library is a monumental shrine to both Ryotaro and the written word, reminiscent of a fantastical European library or a monumental repository for a collection of the world's wisdom.

In 2001, famed architect Tadao Ando constructed this mesmerising vision, one of the final words on libraries and architecture, built in a residential suburb next to where Ryotaro lived and worked. A rotunda in wood, concrete and glass, the building, from the outside, has a deceptively municipal feel. Stroll the internal walkway which affords views of the surrounding greenery that reclusive Ryotaro walked while ruminating on the plot points and social philosophy of his next novel. Breaching the inner sanctum, your first impressions are instantaneous and thrilling. Towering above you are 11-metre-high (36-foot) walls of books, featuring some 20,000 tomes at last count, connected by walkways and staircases. Soaring windows in modernist stained glass, each panel a different size, shape and texture, punctuate the room with light. They allow the shelves to be illuminated, a spiritual meeting of the mind and the heavens. Impressive wooden step ladders also act as bookshelves.

We like to set up and settle in at one of the workspaces using Ryotaro's creative spirit as our inspiration while we work. For extra encouragement, there is also a small exhibit of the cosy room where Ryotaro worked later in life.

南昌荘

13-46 Shimizu-cho,
Morioka-shi, Iwate

Morioka station, then
walk (20min)

NANSHOSO
MORIOKA CITY

The capital city of the Iwate prefecture, Morioka is known for crafts (in particular ironware) but, most importantly to us, is home to our friend Makiko. A relaxed town with historical backstreets, it's a great place for a stroll, particularly along the river under the watchful eye of Mount Iwate, the Fuji of the north.

Nanshoso was officially put onto our must-visit list when Michelle saw some images of the Meiji-period (1868 to 1912) residence. It was once owned by Yasugoro Sekawa, a copper magnate known as 'the mining king'. The protected residence sits near the Kitakami river in quiet and unassuming backstreets. We three visited one summer's day and walked the stone path to the Kanji-emblazoned entrance where warm, dark woods play against white plaster under a gabled, tiled roof.

Inside, wood floors were polished to a gleam; we slipped off our shoes and padded quietly along the corridors. One beautiful room led to another. Walls were bedecked with Meiji-period art and corners propped with ornaments. We paused for tea and wagashi (Japanese sweets), remarking on the chawan (matcha bowls) while gazing out of the rows of beautiful windows overlooking a stunning pond garden with a central winding path.

As famous as the house, the garden is tranquil with small stone bridges and huts popping out amongst the vibrant green of the garden, which is known to be resplendent in the winter snows and the spirit-lifting colours of autumn. We were told by the lovely staff to visit again in hanami (cherry blossom season) to see the blooming of the sakura (cherry blossoms), which must look truly spectacular through the windows.

吉野山

Yoshino-cho, yoshino-gun, Nara
yoshinoyama-sakura.jp
Yoshino station, then ropeway
or walk (8min)

MOUNT YOSHINO
YOSHINO, NARA

There are many places to witness the splendour of sakura (cherry blossoms) during Japan's hanami (cherry blossom season), but the best known among the Japanese people is Nara's Mount Yoshino. Imagine a whole mountain awash with pink, a sea of vibrant blossoms as far as the eye can see. The sight lightens the heart and is colour therapy and nature combined. Accessible from both Kyoto and Osaka, the mountain has over 30,000 cherry trees in 250 different varieties.

Hanami begins around mid-March and reaches full bloom in mid-April. There are four senbon (meaning '1000'), each marking the viewing of 1000 cherry trees. The small 'base camp', Shimo Senbon, is lined with shops, inns and hotels and souvenir stands and begins the festivities, with startling explosions of pink lining the streets on the walk towards the mountain. Naka Senbon (the middle part) and Kami Senbon (upper level) each have an eagle's view of the mountain in its bright pink overcoat. The higher you go on the mountain, the later the blooms. Hanayagura viewpoint on Kami Senbon has the mountain's most spectacular view. Final stage Oku Senbon has less blooms but enjoys the advantage of blooming late. We like to pack a picnic and head to Naka Senbon park and toast the blossoms with a sake or two. Don't forget to make the most of the season and enjoy the themed food, in particular the sakura soft-serve and wagashi (Japanese sweets). Hardcore hikers can climb to the highest point, some 25 kilometres (15 miles) in all, and you'll need to set aside three hours or more. Most people just decide on a 'stage'. Don't put any pressure on yourself, there's plenty to see along the way.

At dusk, everything is illuminated to enhance the beauty, and ultimately it's all one big festival of pink. It's worth noting that although the sakura are the mountain's claim to fame, it also shines in autumn, and in summer hydrangeas dress the mountain in a vibrant blue. In winter the snow adds atmosphere to the mountain shrines and temples.

池田屋安兵衛商店

1-3-5 Tsutsumichodori
Toyama

Toyama Station tram to
Nishicho, then walk (3min)

IKEDA YASUBEI SHOTEN
TOYAMA

A coastal city perched on the mouth of the Sea of Japan on Honshu's mid-western edge, Toyama is home to outstanding food (especially the seafood and fried chicken in black soy sauce), a notable folk craft village and glass museum, and Ikeda Yasubei Shoten, a unique historical pharmacy. A visit had been on Michelle's wishlist for some time, as the Edo-period (1603 to 1867) packaging is fascinating.

Catch one of the trams that rattle their way out of Toyama station to arrive at the striking Edo façade in the heart of the city. Inside the shop evokes the classic story of the Etchu Toyama no Okigusuri, peddlers who manufactured and transported herbal medicines in times gone by. The atmosphere of an old pharmacy remains with high ceilings and wooden beams and the gentle smell of herbal remedies hanging in the air. Displays include colourful medicine boxes and a rare medicine-making machine where you can press and roll the small herbal pellets yourself. A working pharmacy, you can order herbal remedies which are made for you in-house by pharmacists trained in traditional medicine. Powders are weighed out, leaves crushed and tinctures brewed. An in-house restaurant serves food enhanced with medicinal herbs.

Their quirky products make perfect presents. Stock up on herbal tea or remedies for sprains and pains and don't leave without some Etchu-hangontan, Ikeda Yasubei's famous stomach-ache powder. The retro herbal packaging with quirky Edo illustrations of people with various aches and ailments is a wonderful glimpse into the history of Japanese mindfulness and wellness from 200 years ago.

MINDFUL TIP

For the early-medicine curious, the nearby Kokando Pharmacy Museum has some fascinating exhibitions.

立石寺 山寺

4456-1 Yamadera, Yamagata
Yamadera station, then walk to
base of mountain (10min)

RISSHAKUJI TEMPLE (YAMADERA)
YAMADERA, YAMAGATA

As the proverb goes, 'A journey of a thousand miles begins with a single step', and this was our mantra, changing 'miles' to 'steps' as we climbed the mountain to Risshakuji. The Buddhist Tendai sect temple from 860 CE actually has 1015 steps (but who's counting!), winding up through dense forest, past stone statues, lanterns and natural forest and rock formations. The pilgrimage is a true test of the devout (it is said that your earthly desires fall away with each step) or those of us seeking a temple with a spectacular view.

The temple's huge sloping roof is an arresting sight ensconced in the thick fronds of the forest greenery. Even more startling is the Nokyodo Sutra Repository, an ancient dark red building perched precariously on an angular outcrop of jutting rock set against a panoramic backdrop of misty mountains and distant valleys. The Godaido viewing platform gives you a god's eye view of the breathtaking sweep of green.

Those who can't make the journey can still enjoy the small village at the base of the mountain. From the quaint station you see around 30 temples and shrines tenaciously clutching on to the sheer stone faces of the mountain. Dine on the local specialties of soba noodles and afterwards have a soft-serve ice-cream in sweet potato or edamame bean flavours. Don't forget to buy one of the small Jizu statues, the protector of travellers. Take him home and put him on your desk to remind you of your adventure.

Poet Basho made the pilgrimage to Yamadera, and it was here that he composed one of his best-known haiku:

this silence
sinking into rocks
voice of cicada

JAPAN RAIL PASS

A Japan Rail (JR) Pass is great value if you are making more than one long shinkansen (bullet train) trip on your holiday. The price of a Tokyo to Kyoto return trip is a little less than the seven-day rail pass so if you are thinking of catching trains around Japan you can save a lot of money buying this pass.

Set up for non-Japanese citizens, your pass can be purchased before you enter the country (online or through a travel agent) and is valid from a date of your choosing for either seven, 14 or 21 days. You can also buy your pass in Japan for a slightly higher fee. Choose from regular class or green class (a kind of business class). You will need to take your receipt to a Japan Rail ticket office (in larger train stations or at the airport) and they will turn it into a pass for you. Your pass cannot be resupplied so take care not to lose it! Allow time to change your receipt over to a pass as there are often queues.

Shinkansen mostly have a few non-reserved carriages, but you are not guaranteed a seat unless you book a ticket. If you are travelling in green class, you must reserve seats as there are no non-reserved seats. The Japan Rail pass is not available on the fastest of all bullet trains, the Nozomi.

Make sure you are always a little early for your train – Japanese trains are known for their punctuality – and study your reserved ticket so you are standing at the right carriage when your train arrives. Some long-haul trains separate halfway through a journey, so you really need to be in the right place to avoid a travel disaster. Many shinkansen have power chargers and they all have toilets on board.

Japan Rail runs most of the fast trains around the country, however Japan also has lots of privately owned railways. Your pass is only valid on Japan Rail's trains. In and around big cities like Tokyo and Kyoto there are many privately owned train lines and in smaller towns there may be more privately owned scenic train routes. Companies who own

train lines where the JR Pass is not valid are: Odakyu, Kintetsu, Keio, Tokyo Metro, Tobu, Tokyu, Keisei, Seibu, Nishitetsu, Nankai, Hankyu, Keihan, Hanshin, Meitetsu and Keikyu.

EKIBEN

One of the true joys of travelling around Japan on trains is eating a bento box and drinking a strange kind of drink while travelling. Eki means station in Japanese and ben is short for bento. Ekiben are available from larger train stations, and we think the best ones are inside the gates. We always get to the station half an hour early to spend time choosing the right one, and will often plan trips around mealtimes. Bento are also available at convenience stores and department stores.

Try choosing an ekiben with packaging that shows a temple or shrine from the city you are visiting; it means the bento will feature the region's specialties. If you are vegetarian look out for a yasai (vegetable) bento or choose a lunch of onigiri (rice balls) with umeboshi (sour plum) filling or a whole tamago (egg) or vegetable or seaweed fillings. Some shinkansen have a food service where you can buy your ekiben, snacks and drinks on board.

TAXIS

Taxi ranks can be found outside train stations, bus terminals and larger shops. Available taxis will have illuminated signs at night. Check a sign in the corner of the front window. Free is 空車 and may be coloured red; full is 賃 走 or 実 車 and may be coloured green. It will cost around ¥500 to ¥700 for 2 kilometres (1.2 miles), then around ¥80 to ¥90 for every 300 to 400 metres (1000 to 1300 feet) after that. Try to be friendly – a simple hello (konnichiwa) when you enter helps. If you have an address written in Japanese, the driver can put it into their satellite navigation. There is no need to tip, but you can round up.

STAYING IN A RYOKAN

Although Japan offers a range of accommodation options for all budgets, we highly recommend you experience at least one ryokan on your trip. A ryokan is a traditional Japanese inn that provides one or two specially prepared meals (dinner can be served in your room in some establishments) and a bathing experience. Each guest room is decorated in traditional Japanese style, with tatami floors and a central table. The check-in hours and mealtimes are strict, and some ryokan have a curfew. Staying at a ryokan is an unforgettable experience. We love to do it for birthdays, anniversaries and other special occasions.

Ryokan can be anywhere up to 500 years old. The experience includes sleeping in a traditional Japanese room on a futon and taking a hot-springs bath, either in your room or in one of the sex-segregated baths within the ryokan (there can be inside and outside baths).

After dinner, your room will be turned down with cosy futons and pillows. Some ryokan now have modern rooms if you prefer to sleep in a bed. We always look for one with a private reservable bath, or one with a hot-springs bath in the room. The price of staying in a ryokan can seem expensive, but don't forget to factor the meals into the cost.

MONEY

Japan's currency is the yen, denoted by ¥. It comes in denominations of ¥1000, ¥2000, ¥5000 and ¥10,000 in notes, and ¥1, ¥5, ¥10, ¥50, ¥100 and ¥500 in coins. The ¥5 and ¥50 coins have holes in the middle of them.

There is a 10 per cent consumption tax in Japan except on food, drink and newspaper subscriptions which attract an 8 per cent tax. This is sometimes included in the listed price but often isn't, so check first. Sometimes a 'service charge' is added – for hotels and restaurants this can really stack up. Make sure you're aware of any additional costs before making a purchase.

Not all ATMs (cash machines) take international cards, so if you need cash, try a Seven Bank. You'll find Seven Banks in 7-Elevens and in separate outlets. International ATMs can be found in some large stores and department stores, as well as in most post offices.

CONVENIENCE STORES

In Japan, convenience stores are known as konbini and are brilliant pit stops for all your needs. Apart from an impressive range of food and drink, you can buy underwear, hand towels, deodorants, face creams, sunscreen, phone chargers and more, depending on the size and location of the store.

EATING AND DRINKING

Make sure you check the opening hours of your desired cafe or restaurant. Most cafes and bars shut for one day during the week and many cafes open around 11am or 12pm. Lunch starts at 11.30am and finishes between 2 and 3pm. Make sure you know when last orders are as you may miss out otherwise.

Lunch sets are great value, especially at places that do an expensive dinner. It's good fun to try the omakase (chef's choice) at restaurants – the chefs decide what they think is the best choice for you. Many small eateries have plastic food models at the front of their establishment and many cafes have pictorial menus that are very handy if you don't speak Japanese. You can show a staff member the menu and point to your preferred dish. If you don't speak Japanese, ask your hotel to make restaurant reservations on your behalf. Most places are licenced.

When using chopsticks don't stick them upright in a bowl of rice as this is a funeral custom; also, don't pass food to or take food from other people using chopsticks and don't spear food with them (okay, we may have done this a few times); lastly, don't use chopsticks to move a bowl towards you. It's customary to pour other people's drinks before your own.

Tipping is not a thing in Japan, in fact it will cause confusion.

T
R
A
V
E
L

T
I
P
S

VENDING MACHINES

Drink vending machines are found everywhere and the variety of drinks is plentiful. In winter you can choose hot drink options as well as cold, and you may even see small tins of hot soup.

SHOPPING

When you enter a shop or restaurant, staff will say 'irasshaimase' (you are welcome). There's not really an answer to this but sometimes it's so emphatic you'll feel like saying something in return. Just say 'konichiwa' (hello).

Carry your passport with you so that if you purchase something worth over ¥10,000 in major department stores or stores that have a tax-free sign, it can be bought duty free. Do not haggle in Japan unless you are at an open-air market. The consumption tax is now 10 per cent on most items except food and drink and will often be added to prices when paying. Many larger stores and some smaller ones have a tax-back service, which can be especially handy on pricier items.

BINS AND RECYCLING

Consider buying some reusable chopsticks and taking a reusable water bottle and container so you don't use too many single-use items. And don't forget to take your reusable shopping bag so as to not create too much waste.

Bins are not that common in Japan so when you see one dispose of your rubbish. When you find a bin it will often have many recycle options including PET bottles (yellow), combustible/burnable rubbish (red), bottles and cans (blue) and plastics (green).

MANNERS

Manners are very important in Japan so always be as polite as possible. Treat everyone with respect – and respect will be returned to you. The deeper someone bows, the more respect they're showing you. Most younger people don't bow so much now, but a slight nod of the head never goes astray.

Take off your shoes before going into an area with tatami mats or entering a house. A lot of restaurants will also require you to remove your shoes but the staff will let you know (there are usually slippers provided but these are for going to the bathroom). You don't have to worry about this in more contemporary restaurants. You often need to take your shoes off when entering a clothing store changing room.

If you're sick, it is etiquette to wear a face mask.

Don't take a wet umbrella into a shop, use the bags or holders provided.

USEFUL WEBSITES

hyperdia.com Plan your shinkansen trips here. Print your journeys out then take them to a Japan Rail counter to book your tickets.

japaneseguesthouses.com A brilliant resource for booking ryokan accommodation.

jnto.go.jp Japan Tourism's official website, with lots of great information.

kyoto.travel/en A wonderful resource for travel in Kyoto.

dewasanzan.com The Three Mountains of Dewa.

LANGUAGE

Please *see* p. 214 for a handy Japanese language guide to health-related concerns.

Pronunciation

Vowels are:
'a' (pronounced like the 'u' in up)
'i' (pronounced like the 'i' in imp)
'u' (pronounced as the 'oo' in book)
'e' (pronounced as the 'e' in egg)
'o' (pronounced as the 'o' in lock)

This doesn't change for any word. If two vowels are placed together, you say them as two separate, consecutive vowel sounds. Simple! The letter 'r' is pronounced as a cross between an 'r' and an 'l'; the easiest way to make this sound is to touch the roof of your mouth with the tip of your tongue.

Useful Japanese characters

Japan 日本	Tokyo 東京
Station 駅	Yen 円
Male 男	Female 女
Enter 入口	Exit 出口
North 北	South 南
East 東	West 西

Phrase guide

Do you speak English?
Eigo o hanashimasu ka?

I don't understand.
Wakarimasen.

Hello
Konnichiwa

Good morning
Ohayou gozaimasu

Good night
Oyasuminasai

Goodbye
Sayonara

See you later
Mata ne

Nice to meet you
Hajimemashite

Please
Dozo (usually used when offering rather than asking)

Thank you
Arigato or arigato gozaimasu

Thank you very much
Domo arigato

Excuse me
Sumimasen

How are you?
Genki desu ka?

I'm well
Genki desu or genki

How much is this?
Ikura desu ka?

Delicious
Oishii

Can I have the bill please?
Okanjo onegaishimasu?

Taxi
Takushi

Cheers!
Kanpai!

It was quite a feast!
Gochisousama deshita!
(For eating after a delicious meal.)

I love onsen!
Watashi wa onsen ga daisuki!

I don't understand Japanese.
Nihongo ga wakarimasen.

JAPAN TRAVEL IN THE TIME OF COVID-19

At the time of writing, the world is in the grip of the COVID pandemic. It's certain that travel will be possible again, albeit more challenging. Here we have included some tips for you to navigate Japan and seek health advice, should you need it.

Travelling around Japan

In Japan people are very respectful of personal space, however many public places can be crowded. If possible avoid subways and tourist attractions in peak times. Visit tourist attractions midweek instead of the weekend.

Shinkansen (bullet trains) are by reservation only and are always cleaned thoroughly before you embark.

Eating and drinking

You can limit your time spent eating out by buying some fresh fruit for breakfast.

Choose a bed and breakfast package if your accommodation offers breakfast in your room.

If you are worried about eating in crowded places, pack a picnic lunch and spread out in nature in one of Japan's gorgeous green spaces.

T R A V E L   T I P S

Health help

Make sure to research your travel insurance properly and choose a policy that is right for you.

In large cities koban (police boxes) are in and around large intersections and busy places. Try to spot one in your first few days (they look unlike anything in the West). Police are there to help you with anything from directions to any difficulties and will advise you where to go for health advice.

Information booths are in train stations and in many busy places around Japan. They will help you navigate health advice.

Your hotel will also help you to find health advice.

Buy masks in pharmacies and at convenience stores.

Take your own hand sanitiser, buy one at a convenience store or pharmacy or use one when you enter any enclosed space.

Cough into your elbow, or if you think you need to cough, please go outdoors if you can.

Japanese Ministry of Health

The Japanese Ministry of Health has thorough information on COVID-19 including what to do if you are feeling sick or worried about anything. The website includes information on downloading the COCOA App which will notify you if you come into contact with a COVID-positive person.

Information for foreign visitors to Japan
Japan Visitor Hotline (Foreign Language Call Center) 050-3816-2787 (Japanese, English, Chinese and Korean) operated by the Japan National Tourism Organization (JNTO).

www.c19.mhlw.go.jp/covid-19-en.html

Japan National Tourism Organization
JNTO's website has thorough information on COVID-19 and what to do if you are worried about anything.

www.jnto.go.jp/emergency/eng/mi_guide.html

Emergency numbers

These numbers can be called 24 hours a day, 365 days a year, unless otherwise specified.

Police 110

Fire/Ambulance 119

Japan Helpline 0570-000-911

Tokyo Multilingual Call Center
0120-805-261

Police consultation in English
03-3503-8484 (Mon–Fri 8.30am–5.15pm)

Tokyo COVID-19 information
0570-550571 (Mon–Sun 9am–9pm)

Handy Japanese health phrases
Where is the nearest hospital?
Mottomo chikai byōin wa doko desu ka?

Please call an ambulance.
Kyūkyūsha o yonde kudasai.

Where is the nearest pharmacy?
Mottomo chikai isha wa doko desu ka?

I'm not feeling very well.
Kibun ga yokunai or kibun ga warui.

I have a fever.
Netsu ga arimasu.

I have a cough.
Seki ga demasu.

I have a headache.
Atama ga itai desu.

I have a stomach-ache.
Onaka ga itai desu.

The suffixes 'ji' and 'dera' mean temple. The suffix 'en' means garden.

Chawan matcha bowl

Fusuma elegantly painted sliding screens

Geiko or geisha traditional Japanese performing artist and entertainer

Haiku short-verse Japanese poetry

Hanami cherry blossom season

Hina Matsuri Doll's or Girls' Day celebrated on 3 March

Hojicha roasted green tea

Ikebana or kado flower arranging or 'the way of the flower'

Izakaya informal Japanese bar or pub serving small-plate food and drinks

Kaiseki ryori traditional Japanese banquet meal

Kakigori shaved-ice dessert

Kami Shinto spirits or gods

Kanji Chinese script used in Japanese language

Katomado flower-shaped window

Kintsugi golden repair, repairing broken pottery with gold (the art of visible repair)

Kissaten retro coffee house

Kodo appreciation of incense

Kokedama moss ball

Maiko apprentice geisha or geiko

Machiya traditional wooden townhouse

Mingei folk crafts

Momiji autumn leaves

Noren traditional fabric hung over entrances or as room dividers

Omotenashi whole-hearted hospitality

Onsen hot-springs public or private bath

Rotenburo outside hot-springs bath

Ryokan traditional accommodation which can include tatami mats, food, onsen baths, gardens and communal areas

Sakura cherry blossom

Sencha infused green tea

Sento public bathhouse with regular water (not hot springs water)

Shakkei borrowed scenery

Shinkansen bullet trains

Shinrin yoku forest bathing

Shinto a nature religion, Japan's largest religion

Shoji screens traditional sliding transparent screens

Shojin ryori traditional vegetarian multi-course meal often served in Buddhist temples

Shukubo temple lodging

Tatami traditional Japanese flooring mats made from soft rush

Teishoku simple homestyle lunch and dinner sets

Umami a deep and pleasant savoury taste

Wabi-sabi the acceptance of transience and imperfection

Wagashi Japanese sweets

Yuba tofu skin

Yuka highly polished floors

Yukata summer cotton kimono

Zazen Zen-style meditation

Zen Buddhism a sect of the Buddhist religion

TIME PERIODS

Nara and Heian (794 to 1185 CE)

Kamakura (1192 to 1333)

Muromachi (1336 to 1573)

Azuchi-Momoyama (1573 to 1603)

Edo (1603 to 1867)

Meiji (1868 to 1912)

Taisho (1912 to 1926)

Showa (1926 to 1989)

Heisei (1989 to 2019)

Reiwa (2019 to present)

Image credits

All images are © Steve Wide and Michelle Mackintosh, except for the following:

Front cover image, pp. 122-3: HOSHINOYA Fuji; p.IV © Armelle Habib; pp. 41, 148, 198, 199 Shutterstock; pp. 2, 76, 90-1 © Sakurai Kokeshi; p.6 © Hiki Komura; p. 27 © Kenninji Temple; p. 28 © Ninnaji Temple; p. 33 © Σ64, Wikicommons, GNU Free Documentation License.; pp. 34-5 © Hotokuji Temple; pp. 42-3 © Nishinotoin Tea Shop and Motoan Teahouse; p. 45 © 663highland, Wikicommons, GNU Free Documentation License.; pp.46-7 © Taihoan ; p. 48 Nakamura Tokichi Honten © Dick Thomas Johnson Wikicommons Creative Commons Attribution 2.0 Generic license; pp. 38, 50-1 © Tokoan; p. 53 Joan © Suikotei, Wikicommons, Creative Commons Attribution-Share Alike 4.0 International license; pp. 59 bottom right, 69 bottom, © Zao Onsen; p. 61 © Stephanie Rooney; p. 63 © bottom image Sainokawara Park; p. 64 © Genji No Yu; p. 66 Photo 69135058 © Phuongphot, Dreamstime.com; p. 74 © Ryokan Sanga; pp. 80-1 © Yamada-Matsu; p. 82 © Kyoto Shibori Museum; p. 83 © Taizoin Temple; p. 84 © Ikenobo; p. 85 © roberthardin, Alamy Stock Photo; p. 87 top © Takuminosato Craft Village; pp. 88-9 © Minshuku Furuki; p. 93, Lazartiva, iStock Photo; p. 103 © Tocen Goshobo; p. 112, 118-19 © Kishi-Ke; pp. 116-17 © Hotel Wood; pp. 124-5,

155 bottom © Treeful Treehouse; p. 126 © Yasuesou; p. 127 © Minshuku Kanja; pp. 128-9, 155 right © Hatcho No Yu; p. 130 © Forest; p. 131 © SSimon, Wikicommons, Creative Commons Attribution-Share Alike 3.0 Unported license.; pp. 135 top, 144-5 © Kakurinbo Shukubo; pp. 132, 135 top, 136-7 © Shunkoin Temple; pp. 138-9 © Chionin Wajun-Kaikan; p. 142 © Rokuoin Temple; p. 143 Daihonzan Eiheiji Temple ©Tak H, Wikicommons, Creative Commons Attribution-Share Alike 2.0 Generic license.; pp. 146-7 Daishinbo Shukubo © Timothy Bunting; p. 150-1 © Tsushima Seizanji Temple; p. 159 Lukas, Wikicommons, Creative Commons Attribution 2.0 Generic license.; p. 162 Sankeien Garden © 雷太, Wikicommons, Creative Commons Attribution 2.0 Generic license.; p. 163 Koishikawa Korakuen © 公益財団法人 東京都 公園協会, Wikicommons, Creative Commons Attribution 4.0; p. 169 © Yuushien Garden; p. 175 top image © Go! Nagano; p. 177 © Osaka Convention & Tourism Bureau; pp. 178, 189 top, 191 bottom © JNTO; p. 187 © Susann Schuster (Unsplash); p. 189 bottom © Timothy Bunting; p. 191 top © Reggaeman, Wikicommons, Creative Commons Attribution-Share Alike 3.0 Unported license; p. 203 © Shiba Ryotaro Memorial Museum Library; p. 205 © Mount Yoshino © Luka Peternel, Wikicommons Creative Commons Attribution-Share Alike 4.0 International license.

Steve Wide and **Michelle Mackintosh** have been obsessed with Japan since their first visit in the late 1990s. Based in Melbourne, Australia, they now call Japan their 'home away from home', spending at least three months of the year there. Steve is a travel and pop culture writer with a master's degree in creative writing. He has written 10 books on music genres and icons. He also hosts a long running indie radio show on Melbourne's 3RRR FM and has interviewed and DJed with some of the indie scene's most influential bands. Michelle is an award-winning book designer and illustrator. She has also written three books: *Snail Mail*, *Care Packages* and *Sustainable Gifting*. Her work has been exhibited in Tokyo, and she has a wrapping paper range sold in Japan. Together Steve and Michelle have written, designed and illustrated seven books on Japan which have been translated into multiple languages.

We are truly mindful of the wonderful work put into this book by the following people. Melissa Kayser, who developed and oversaw our book's concept. To our dream team who worked tirelessly to make sure everything was more than perfect: Megan Cuthbert who project managed, and crafted the detail to design and editing, Alice Barker who fine-tooth combed the writing and masterfully edited, Megan Ellis who expertly crafted and typeset, Rosanna Dutson who meticulously proofread, Hikaru Komura who expertly cleaned up the kanji. Thank you to the following lovely people for generous help with pictures and details: Yuko Fujii from Gunma Prefectural Government, Yuka Shimizu and Yusuke Harada from Hoshinoya Resorts, Alison Roberts-Brown the official representative in Australia for the Kyoto City Tourism Association, Tourism Garden Pty Ltd, Timothy Bunting from https://dewasanzan.com, Vincent Penez from Japanese Guest Houses, Osaka Info, Hiki Komura, Makiko Sugita and to all the venues who generously supplied imagery. Thank you to Miss Jane for her pep-talks, and as always thank you to our family, Japanese family and friends whose love, generosity and support means the world to us. RIP Bronte, your mindful romping in our Japanese garden will be forever treasured in our memories.

Published in 2022 by Hardie Grant Explore, an imprint of Hardie Grant Publishing

Hardie Grant Explore (Melbourne)
Wurundjeri Country
Building 1, 658 Church Street
Richmond, Victoria 3121

Hardie Grant Explore (Sydney)
Gadigal Country
Level 7, 45 Jones Street
Ultimo, NSW 2007

www.hardiegrant.com/au/explore

A catalogue record for this book is available from the National Library of Australia

Hardie Grant acknowledges the Traditional Owners of the Country on which we work, the Wurundjeri people of the Kulin Nation and the Gadigal people of the Eora Nation, and recognises their continuing connection to the land, waters and culture. We pay our respects to their Elders past and present.

Mindfulness Travel Japan
ISBN 9781741177237

10 9 8 7 6 5 4 3 2 1

Publisher
Melissa Kayser

Project editor
Megan Cuthbert

Editor
Alice Barker

Proofreader
Rosanna Dutson

Japanese language advisor
Hikaru Komura

Design
Michelle Mackintosh

Typesetting
Megan Ellis

Index
Max McMaster

Colour reproduction by Megan Ellis and Splitting Image Colour Studio

Printed and bound in China by LEO Paper Products LTD.